# EXIT READY

# EXIT
# READY

---

## THE PROVEN SYSTEM TO EXIT
## ANY BUSINESS AT
## THE RIGHT TIME FOR THE
## MAXIMUM PRICE

BY

**ROLAND FRAISER**

Copyright © 2025 Roland Frasier

All rights reserved. No part of this book may be reproduced or used in any manner without the prior written permission of the copyright owner, except for the use of brief quotations in a book review.

To request permissions, contact the publisher at publisher@scalable.co.

ISBN 979-8-9886737-6-7 (hardcover)
ISBN 979-8-9886737-4-3 (paperback)
ISBN 979-8-9886737-7-4 (audiobook)
ISBN 979-8-9886737-5-0 (ebook)

First Scalable edition, November 2025.

Editing by Erin MacPherson, Andy Rogers, and Phil Newman
Layout by Immaculate Studios
Supplemental interior changes by Taylor Nelson

Printed by IngramSpark.

The Scalable Company
4330 Gaines Ranch Loop, Suite 120
Austin, TX 78735

https://www.scaleandexit.com/

# CONTENTS

A Note to the Reader                                    1

Introduction                                            5

**Part 1 - Your Crash course on Exits**               13

    Chapter 1: Understanding Exits                    15

    Chapter 2: Understanding Your Number              41

    Chapter 3: Understanding Multiples                55

    Chapter 4: Understanding Levels of Risk           81

**Part 2 - Getting Exit-Ready**                        95

    Chapter 5: Getting Exit-Ready                     97

**Part 3 - Actually Making Your Exit**                183

    Chapter 6: Planning Your Exit                    185

    Chapter 7: The Right Exit Process for You        197

    Chapter 8: Finding a Buyer for Your Business     211

    Chapter 9: Executing Your Exit                   231

**Appendix: Some Final Advice on Exiting**            243

# A NOTE TO THE READER

Welcome to *Exit Ready!*

This book is here to help owners of small- and medium-sized business like you understand how to exit your business when the time comes. Even if you're not thinking about exiting right now, it's smart to know how it works so you're ready when it happens.

## Why Think About Exiting Now?

Eventually, everyone exits their business, one way or another. Planning ahead means you can do it your way and get the best deal possible. If something unexpected happens, being prepared helps you handle it better.

## What's in This Book?

The vital subjects we'll talk about include:

- Whether (and when) your exit makes strategic sense
- Knowing what your business is worth beforehand
- Deciding who will run the business after you
- Selling at the highest price on the best possible terms

- Making sure all of the legal requirements are met

- . . . and much more.

Along the way, we'll share not only relevant ideas and recommendations but also compelling stories from real-world exits to show how things work. In some places we had to change names and details due to confidentiality agreements, but every lesson in this book is real, and they all come from years in the trenches doing actual deals.

## A Big Thank-You

This book wouldn't be here without my business partners, Ryan Deiss and Richard Lindner, and our amazing team of people both inside our companies and in the book creating, editing, and publishing world. They worked hard to make the concepts, insights, and lessons within these pages come to life, and I couldn't have done it without them.

## Why I Wrote This Book

I've personally helped with over one thousand business exits, from small local shops to big international conglomerates. While each exit is unique, a number of sound principles and practices that make the process successful have emerged over the years. I have felt increasingly compelled to share what my team and I have learned to help you get ready to exit your business. While the prospect of letting go and handing the reins of your operation to another can feel daunting, the insights we have assembled in this book are designed to guide you toward executing your own exit with a clear sense of purpose and a high level of confidence.

When you're ready, we hope you'll think about working with us as advisors or partners to make your exit the best it can be. Exiting your business is a big step. But with good planning, you can make sure it goes smoothly and meets your goals.

Let's get started on this journey together.

Best wishes,

**Roland Frasier**
San Diego, California

# INTRODUCTION
## LET'S GET EXIT-READY

The offer came out of nowhere. Mike was obsessively focused on growing his business and providing his customers with the best service possible, as he had done for the past eight years. He had never even considered the possibility that someone might want to buy his business.

But there it was in black and white. It had started a few weeks earlier, when one of his competitors reached out and asked for an appointment. He explained that they had just hired a new CEO and were building their business to sell, hopefully to a large private equity fund that would grow it even more and possibly even take the whole thing public a few years later.

Understandably, Mike was skeptical about this outreach. He couldn't help thinking that this competitor might just be fishing for information about Mike's business to then use it to compete against him. But curiosity got the better of him, and he agreed to set the appointment.

During the meeting, the founder of Mike's competitor (let's call them Global Services Company or "GSC") explained the strategy. They had enjoyed strong growth for several years and were now focused on how they might exit the business to pursue other ventures or possibly enter retirement.

Their three-point plan was to 1) hire seasoned operational executives to replace the founder team, 2) professionalize the business with standard operating procedures and proven management systems, and 3) grow dramatically through a series of acquisitions. Ideally, the first acquisition would be Mike's company.

Having been focused for so long on survival and then growth and customer service, Mike had never really stopped to consider selling, and now he had someone telling him they wanted to buy his business. A number of initial thoughts arose in his mind.

*How much was his business worth?*

*What would he do after the sale if he did accept an offer?*

*What would happen to his employees, his customers, and his legacy?*

These were all new questions, and Mike needed someone to help get him the answers before he went any further down this road.

That's when he called me. Mike had heard me speaking about buying and selling businesses at several conferences, and we'd happened to reconnect when he randomly sat next to me on a flight from Las Vegas to San Diego just a month before GSC's inquiry about buying his business.

Mike was fortunate to have someone to talk with about the possibility of selling. Many business owners receive calls and contacts from potential buyers and go through the full process of selling their business without ever having the benefit of an advisor who has been through the process multiple times, one who knows all the pitfalls and opportunities that sellers encounter during the process.

Many of them never consider the importance of maximizing the value of their business, and they end up leaving millions of dollars on the table— money they could have received if they just knew more about the major steps necessary to get their businesses "Exit-Ready."

Mike and I chatted, and he retained me to help him navigate the process. He introduced me to the GSC team. We secured an NDA (non-disclosure agreement) to protect each of our sensitive and confidential information. We talked through what Mike's "number" might be—the minimum he would need to receive to consider a sale—and then we began the conversation with GSC in earnest.

As a result of going through the potential buyer's acquisition process, we determined that a sale at that time should provide Mike with about $15 million.

We also discovered that, given Mike's then-current Exit Unreadiness, he would likely receive significantly more from a sale if we completed my full Exit-Ready process to plug the valuation gaps in his business, making it more valuable and also more appealing to a wider group of potential buyers.

Mike wisely decided to pass on the opportunity to sell to GSC, and we partnered up to implement the Exit-Ready process in his business with the goal of selling within five years. Two years later, we received an offer valued at approximately $180 million from a private equity firm.

At that point, however, we were on a growth spurt and were still completing major upgrades to Mike's business. We had hired a CFO (Chief Financial Officer) and financial professionals to build the finance team. We added a CMO (Chief Marketing Officer) to grow sales by tapping new customer acquisition channels the company had ignored as it grew.

We also acquired a company that provided services to our customers that Mike's company had been outsourcing for several years. The company we acquired grew about ten times larger in that two-year period than it was when we bought it.

Imagine what would have happened if Mike had sold his business to the first company that expressed interest in buying it. He would have left about $165 million on the table!

Granted, he would have had $15 million in cash, but taking the time to get professional advice, implement the Exit-Ready process, and focus on professionalizing and optimizing the business to be Exit-Ready made the difference between a solid exit payday and a life-changing, generational wealth opportunity.

Ultimately, Mike decided to pass on the $180 million opportunity as well, because he could see that the company had momentum and was on a path to hitting our target valuation of $500 million once we completed all our Exit-Ready process initiatives.

What I want for you to take away from this example—and from reading this book—is that it makes sense to plan for an exit long before anyone comes along to make you an offer to buy your business. In doing so, you will only make the business stronger, more profitable, and more valuable for yourself, even if you never decide to sell.

The truth is that you should always be in the process of exiting.

No matter where you are in your business lifecycle, and no matter what you're doing, it's wise to think of yourself as being in the process of exiting. Why? Because your business was created to serve you. That's right: It may be your passion, your dream, your life's work, but it was still created with an end goal in mind: to serve you.

That said, you will exit one day. Even if you stay working until the day you die, you will exit. When you do, what will happen to your business?

What will happen to the people who work there? What will happen to your family? What about your customers and your products? And what about your bank accounts? Will you be able to live the lifestyle you desire after you exit? Will your kids be provided for? Will you be able to invest in causes that matter to you?

It's good to start asking all of these questions as soon as you can—that way, you can prepare yourself and your business to reach all of your goals.

Think of it this way: Let's say you start a business when you're thirty-five, and it goes gangbusters. By the time you're forty, it's bringing in $10 million in revenue each year, you have one hundred employees, and your product line is expanding at a rate such that you expect the revenue trajectory to double in five years.

Five years later, you're forty-five, you have a business that earns more than $25 million annually, with two hundred employees. You're netting a hefty $3 million a year, which means you are able to afford the best schools, a gorgeous house, fantastic vacations, and even a little house by the beach where your family can get away.

Things are going great for you. So when should you start planning your exit?

Most people say it depends on your "number." That is how much you would be willing to sell the business for if someone wanted to buy it from you.

The number is important, but there is a danger in waiting until you have it nailed down to start thinking about getting your business Exit-Ready. Why? Because at that point, you will very likely not have the time you need to prepare your business for sale in a way that ensures you get the maximum valuation at the sale.

That's what the Exit-Ready process is designed to do. It's a process that you ideally put into place today, long before the offers start to come in.

Don't get me wrong: I am not suggesting that you should sell your business right now if you are happy with how things are going. If things are going well and you have not yet achieved a valuation for the business that will get your "number", then you should stay, keep that momentum going, keep growing, keep doing great things.

But if you follow the Exit-Ready process, you'll learn that while you're growing, you should also make a plan to exit. You should think about how much you need from your exit to maintain your desired lifestyle for the rest of your life—how much you need to do the things you want to do. You should consider the five types of exits (which we'll discuss in chapter 1), figure out how to grow your profit margins, and think about strategic mergers and acquisitions (M&A) so your business will be all set for your exit at the highest possible valuation.

You should also consider how you can stop being the face of your business so that someone else can take over for you. And you should think about how to make your business passive so you can keep making money off of the work you've done, even when you're done doing the work.

I have spent the last thirty-plus years working as an entrepreneur. I've started, bought, sold, acquired, and scaled dozens of businesses myself and advised on over a thousand different transactions. Some of them turned into huge enterprises that allowed me to realize huge returns when I exited, and others crashed and burned.

Along the way, I've learned a lot about when, why, and how to exit. I know:

- how to get a business ready to exit,

- how owners can maximize the valuation of a company to get the money they need when they exit,

- how to appeal to the largest possible group of buyers to create an auction where multiple buyers are bidding for the privilege of acquiring your business, and

- how to negotiate and structure the deal to maximize your take-home cash from the sale.

Getting a business Exit-Ready is hard work and generally a two-to-five-year process. But if it's done right, you can maximize the sales price and get enough out of the business to do the things you want to do for the long term. Maybe you want to buy or start another business, or maybe you want to retire to the beach. Either way, by being Exit-Ready, you will be well on the way to reaching your goals.

So, what are your goals? What do you want to do with your life and business in the next year? Five years? Ten years? Twenty? It's time to figure out where you're heading, and what you need to do to get there.

It's time to get **Exit-Ready.**

## Part

# One

# YOUR CRASH COURSE ON EXITS

CHAPTER 1

# UNDERSTANDING EXITS

I can't tell you how many times someone has told me that so-and-so got *this many* millions for selling their business, or that they had just talked to a business founder who exited for seven, eight, or nine figures.

They always assume two things about that situation.

The first assumption is that the person who sold actually received the full amount of the sales price. The second is that the person who sold is a genius at exiting and therefore would make the perfect advisor to help anyone else who wants to sell their business.

Generally, both of those assumptions are completely incorrect. Take Rand Fishkin, for example. He and his mother founded an SEO business, Moz. In 2016, a financing round valued the company at about $120 million (pre-money). To most of the outside world, Rand was a business genius and worth at least tens of millions of dollars. However, after multiple financing rounds, his ownership interest had dropped to roughly 20 percent of the common stock, and when Moz was ultimately acquired by iContact in 2021, the price was not disclosed. Fishkin has written that he no longer controlled the company by the end, that he's legally barred from revealing the sale amount, and that while his personal proceeds were "life-changing," they were lower than he would have received from an earlier, signed 2019 deal around $90 million that never closed.[1]

Rand is exceptionally honest and transparent about the challenges he faced as an owner and seller of a business. He is also forthright in sharing just how many mistakes he made along the way. The point is that most of the people I talk to who brag about exiting a business received substantially less from the sale than they could have received, mostly because, while they are good at whatever business they created, they had little to no knowledge or experience with respect to the process of preparing a business for sale at the highest price, negotiating the best price, or running an exit process.

To truly understand exits, you need more than one or two or three exits under your belt, and you need to be present for all of the negotiations and dealmaking that goes on throughout the exit process. I have been the founder, owner, attorney, financial expert, operations expert, marketing expert, negotiator, tax advisor, investment banker, and/or acquisition strategist on more exits than I can count. There are dozens of opportunities that most experts miss when preparing a company for sale (the Exit-Ready process), running the process, negotiating and contracting the sale, completing the deal through closing, and post-sale integration and related issues.

Only a few people have experience in all of these disparate areas, and who therefore have the insight to help you truly understand all of the many levers you can pull to increase your ultimate take-home proceeds from the sale of your business.

---

1 Rand Fishkin, "The Final Chapter of My First Startup," *SparkToro Blog*, October 26, 2023; Rand Fishkin, "My Last Day at Moz. My First Day at SparkToro," *SparkToro Blog*, February 27, 2018; John Cook, "Moz raises $10M from Foundry Group at $120M valuation," *GeekWire*, January 20, 2016; Taylor Soper, "SEO software startup Moz acquired by iContact Marketing Corp., 17 years after launching in Seattle," *GeekWire*, June 4, 2021.

This Crash Course section of the book is designed to give you a peek into the many different areas of the Exit-Ready process so that you have a solid grasp on all that it entails.

Do you know someone who likes to read the last page of a novel first? Maybe that's you. Last-page readers like to know how the story ends, which character wins their love interest, and which spends the rest of their life in jail *before* they commit to reading the whole book. But last-page readers have no idea how the characters got where they got.

The lesson here is that knowing where the characters end up doesn't mean you understand *how* things happened in the story. It doesn't mean you *know* the characters and what the heck they were doing way down by the lake at 2 a.m. on a Monday. It takes reading the book to figure out the story that led to the ending.

Let's imagine ourselves as last-page readers, but we're not reading a novel. We're looking at the story of your business. After reading the last page, you know the ending—an exit from your business that helps you to reach your personal, professional, and financial goals—so now we're going to start at the beginning of the story. We're going to go back to chapter one and figure all that out.

One thing I've learned is that it's pretty hard to work toward something—in this case, an exit—without understanding what it is. So that's where we will start. You may know some of this—or even all of it—but I want give you a clear, concrete picture of what an exit is and of what it means to build an Exit-Ready business.

## The Sales, Profit, Value Model

For a business to be Exit-Ready, it has to have *transferable* value. Essentially, it needs to be worth something, not just to you but to other people.

You may be thinking, *Doesn't every business have transferable value?* Well, not necessarily. For example, a friend of mine inherited a family business that restored, refinished, and sold antique cars. The business made lots of sales, and therefore profits, so when my friend  tiinherited it, the operation owned millions of dollars' worth of antique car parts, as well as dozens of partially restored vehicles. One problem: My friend's deceased father was one of the few people in the entire world with the skill set to repair and restore those particular cars the way their customers wanted. So, what seemed like a very valuable business ended up being worth very little to my friend because there was no one he could transfer the value to.

Another business owner, a former client of my law firm, contacted me and said he and his wife were ready to sell the electronic equipment e-commerce store they'd built together. While it was a $60 million a year business, unfortunately the business depended on both of them for all of its operations. It also depended on his wife's minority business owner status to maintain its slim profit margins. Once we went through the numbers of what the business would be worth to a potential buyer, the amount was so small they couldn't afford to sell.

To avoid a similar situation, the very first thing to understand when you're working to build an Exit-Ready business is transferable value and how that transferable value interacts with other parts of your business. The model I use to describe, and then create, transferable value is what I call SPV, which stands for sales, profit, value.

To understand the SPV model, start by thinking about the correlation between *leveraged sales* and *bankable profits*.

Most businesses focus on sales but never really think about how to get the most from every sale they make to a customer. Here's a primer on what leveraged sales are so that you can see why they are so important to your business.

Many businesses fixate on generating sales without fully considering how to maximize the value extracted from each customer interaction. This is where the concept of leveraged sales comes in: transforming a business's approach from simply closing deals to building a dynamic and self-amplifying sales engine. Leveraged sales are not merely about increasing sales volume; they are about amplifying the impact of each sale through strategic relationships and intelligent selling techniques.

At the heart of leveraged sales lies the power of partnerships. These partnerships can be broadly categorized into channel partners and strategic partners. Channel partners act as extensions of a company's sales force, effectively multiplying its reach and capacity. This category encompasses a variety of models, each with its own strengths.

Resellers, for example, purchase products at wholesale prices and market them to their own customer base, often adding value through services or customization. Value-Added Resellers (VARs) take this a step further by integrating, implementing, and supporting the products they sell, significantly enhancing the customer offering. Distributors, operating at a larger scale, connect manufacturers with a network of resellers, while dealers may have exclusive rights to sell within specific territories. Retail partners, both online and brick-and-mortar, offer another avenue to reach customers through established retail channels.

Beyond these transactional relationships, strategic partnerships are forged to create mutually beneficial outcomes that extend beyond a simple buy-sell dynamic. Technology partners, for instance, collaborate to integrate their products or services, resulting in a more comprehensive and valuable joint solution—imagine a CRM software seamlessly integrating with an email marketing platform. Original Equipment Manufacturer (OEM) partners embed a company's product into their own, often under a white label, as seen when a software component is integrated into a hardware device. Joint ventures involve two or more companies pooling resources to develop and market a new offering, while co-marketing and co-branding partnerships leverage each other's audiences through collaborative marketing campaigns.

Influencers—individuals or organizations with substantial sway over a target market—can be engaged to promote products to their followers. Finally, partnering with industry organizations and associations provides access to a concentrated audience of businesses or professionals, expanding reach within a specific sector.

Within this framework of partnerships, specific techniques can be employed to maximize revenue generation.

*Upselling* encourages customers, either directly or through partners, to opt for a higher-priced, upgraded, or premium version of a product or service. A well-trained reseller, for instance, might effectively pitch the "Pro" version of a software package over the "Basic" version by highlighting its enhanced features and benefits. Partners should be thoroughly trained and incentivized to upsell, provided with resources such as comparison charts and compelling sales scripts.

*Cross-selling* involves offering complementary products or services alongside the initial purchase. A technology partner, for instance, might offer data migration services when a customer licenses a new software platform. Equipping partners with a deep understanding of the product ecosystem enables them to identify and capitalize on these cross-selling opportunities.

*Downselling,* while less common in purely leveraged models, involves offering a scaled-down or lower-priced version of a product when a customer balks at the initial offering, salvaging a potential sale that might otherwise be lost. Partners must be given clear guidelines on when and how to employ downselling effectively.

*Bundling* combines multiple products or services into a single package, often at a discounted price, to enhance the perceived value and increase the average order value. Strategic partners often create and promote bundles that integrate their respective offerings, creating a compelling proposition for the customer.

*Multiples,* selling multiple licenses or units of a product at a volume discount, can be facilitated by partners who leverage their client relationships to identify buyers in need of bulk purchases.

Beyond these core partner-driven models, other leveraged sales approaches include *affiliate* and referral sales. Affiliate sales leverage the reach of individuals or companies who promote a product and earn a commission on each sale generated through their unique referral links. Bloggers, YouTubers, and website owners can become effective affiliates, essentially acting as an incentivized extension of the marketing team.

Referral sales, on the other hand, rely on the power of word-of-mouth, whereby existing customers or partners refer new business, often in exchange for rewards or incentives. This leverages the trust inherent in existing relationships to acquire new customers at a relatively low cost.

All of that said, building a successful leveraged sales ecosystem requires more than simply establishing partnerships. It demands a strategic and systematic approach. Businesses must begin by identifying their ideal customer profile and then carefully selecting partners who can effectively reach that target audience and align with the overall business goals.

A well-defined partner program should be developed, outlining the benefits, requirements, and expectations of the partnership. Partners need to be recruited, onboarded, thoroughly trained, and provided with marketing materials and ongoing sales support. Joint go-to-market strategies should be created with strategic partners, capitalizing on their expertise and market reach.

Partners must be equipped with the knowledge and tools to effectively upsell, cross-sell, and bundle products. Robust systems should be implemented to track partner performance, including sales, leads generated, and customer satisfaction metrics. Ongoing support and communication are essential to nurture strong partner relationships.

Finally, clear incentives, such as commissions, marketing development funds (MDF), and performance-based bonuses, should be established to motivate partners. Continuous monitoring and optimization of the partner program are critical to ensure it consistently delivers the desired results.

By strategically combining these elements—a diverse range of partnerships, effective revenue-maximization techniques, and a well-structured partner program—businesses can construct a robust leveraged sales ecosystem. This ecosystem, when properly nurtured, can drive significant growth and expand market presence far beyond the capabilities of traditional sales models, ultimately transforming the way a company generates and maximizes its revenue.

A properly implemented leveraged sales system allows companies to grow in a nonlinear fashion, with their partners acting as force multipliers and the company expanding at a pace and cost far superior to what it could do on its own.

Leveraged sales form the first part of the SPV model and the first big opportunity to optimize your business for sale at maximum valuation. That's because the greater the leverage in your sales, the higher your bankable profit is likely to be, which leads us to the second major component of the SPV model, *bankable profit.*

While the term "profit" is frequently celebrated in the business world, a closer examination reveals that not all profits are created equal. A crucial distinction exists between the profit figure that appears on a company's income statement and the portion of that profit that is truly *bankable*—that is, available for the owner to freely utilize without compromising the health or future of the enterprise. Understanding this difference is fundamental to sound financial management and strategic decision-making and forms an integral part of the Exit-Ready model and process.

Profit, in its simplest form, is the result of subtracting total expenses from total revenue. This is the number that forms the basis of many financial analyses and performance evaluations. However, this figure, often referred to as accounting profit, can be misleading when assessing the owner's discretionary income.

Bankable profit, on the other hand, represents the portion of profit that can be safely extracted from the business without jeopardizing its ongoing operations, growth trajectory, or financial stability. It's the actual cash available for the owner's personal use, alternative investments, or any other purpose after all obligations, both present and future, have been considered.

Several factors contribute to the often-significant gap between these two types of profit. One key factor is the presence of banking covenants. Loan agreements frequently stipulate that borrowing companies must maintain specific financial ratios, such as a healthy debt-to-equity ratio or current ratio. These covenants are designed to protect the lender's interests, and violating them can trigger penalties ranging from increased interest rates to, in extreme cases, loan default. Consequently, a portion of the profits might need to be retained within the business to ensure these ratios remain within the acceptable range, bolstering the company's financial position and satisfying lender requirements.

Furthermore, the imperative for growth necessitates reinvesting a substantial portion of profits back into the business. These reinvestment needs encompass various critical areas. Capital expenditures (CapEx) are

required to acquire new equipment, upgrade technology, or expand facilities, all of which are essential for maintaining competitiveness and increasing capacity.

Working capital needs—including funding inventory, managing accounts receivable, and covering day-to-day operational expenses—must also be met to ensure smooth business operations. Investing in research and development (R&D) is crucial for fostering innovation, developing new products, and improving existing ones, thus securing the company's future market position. Finally, expanding marketing and sales initiatives requires funding to fuel growth and reach new markets.

Beyond these operational and growth-related needs, obligations to other stakeholders can further reduce the bankable portion of profits. If the business has multiple owners or shareholders, a predetermined portion of the profits may be contractually obligated for distribution as dividends or profit shares.

Similarly, employee bonuses or profit-sharing plans, while valuable for incentivizing performance and fostering loyalty, can also diminish the pool of bankable profits. Debt service, encompassing both principal and interest payments on outstanding loans, also directly impacts the amount of cash available to the owner.

Finally, the tax liabilities associated with profits must be settled before any remaining amount can be considered truly bankable. Corporate or personal income taxes, depending on the business structure, represent a significant claim on profits that must be satisfied prior to determining the owner's discretionary funds.

In essence, while the profit figure on the income statement provides a snapshot of the company's overall financial performance, it is the bankable profit that reflects the owner's actual financial flexibility. Recognizing the distinction between these two types of profit is not merely an academic exercise; it is essential for making informed decisions about resource allocation, investment strategies, and personal financial planning.

Understanding the factors that constrain bankable profits allows business owners to navigate the complexities of financial management with greater clarity and ensure the long-term health and prosperity of their enterprise, while also having a firm grasp on what their actual discretionary income derived from the business truly is.

At a very basic level, steady and ongoing leveraged sales should result in bankable profits. The sales drive the profits, and the profits, in turn, can be reinvested into the business so you can make more sales. The more profit you make, the more you can spend to get more sales, which, in turn, results in more profit.

The challenge with most businesses I work with is that they are focused on profits, but they are not focused on *bankable* profits.

Sales and profit are Business 101, but sales and profit alone don't equal transferable value. There's something missing from the equation, and that missing piece can make all the difference in whether or not you are Exit-Ready, as evidenced by the story above.

Imagine a Venn diagram. Put sales on one side and profits on the other. Then, add a third circle called transferable value that overlaps with both sales and profits.

**SPV VENN DIAGRAM**

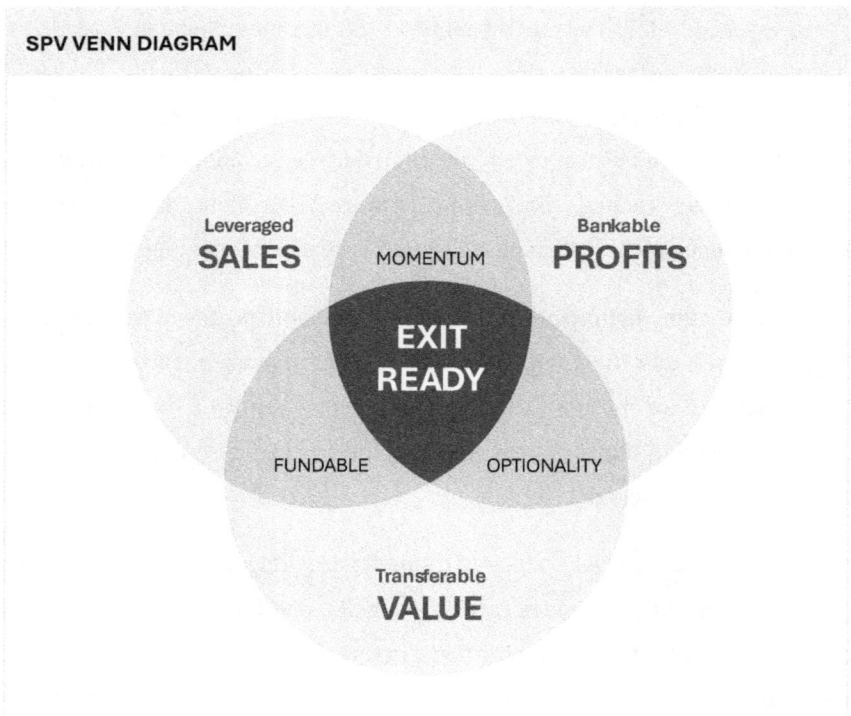

In the place where transferable value and sales overlap, businesses can use that transferable value to raise money to fund sales before they get to profitability. It also allows them to raise money through either debt or equity to amass more capital to invest in growing sales, even above and beyond profits. This overlap gives the business the power to be *fundable*.

On the other side, where bankable profits overlap with transferable value, you have *optionality*. This overlap is where you can sell the business, which is profitable (but hopefully not before implementing the Exit-Ready process), or you can just continue to receive the profits and carry on. The overlap between bankable profits and transferable value gives you the ability to choose—optionality. Do we want to just fund this thing through profits? Do we want to raise money? Do we want to sell? Optionality gives us a lot of choices, and the people who have the most choices tend to be the people who win.

The SPV model is the basic framework this entire book is built upon, and we will refer to it many times. When a business manages to align transferable value, bankable profits, and sales all together, that's when the business is truly Exit-Ready.

## The Exit Amplifiers Tool

One of the tools every founder needs to be Exit-Ready is the Exit Amplifiers Tool. (I often call this the 50 Amplifiers Tool on my podcast and in my courses, so if you're reading this and recognize it, it's one and the same. Since it's a tool that is changing all the time, I'll just call it the Amplifiers Tool, as you may find that there are *more* than fifty by the time that you're reading this.) It will be helpful to have the tool on hand as you read this book, so before going any further, visit https://scalable.co/ExitReadyResources and download yours. Note that the link is to a dot co domain, not dot com.

The Exit Amplifiers tool helps you to identify all the things that can increase (amplify) the value of your ultimate exit. We'll refer to it a few times in this book, so keep it nearby. It will help you plot your exit path.

## The Five Exits of an Entrepreneur

The truth is that we are always exiting something.

A lot of us are what we call *accidental entrepreneurs*; we didn't plan to be an entrepreneur. We didn't set out to be in business or even ever conceive that we might be growing or exiting one. We were just good at something, we started something, and we filled some need. Before we knew it, we found ourselves in business.

But an accidental start doesn't have to mean an accidental end. Here's a tough truth: Everybody exits eventually, one way or the other. Nobody gets to stay in business forever. Nobody will be running their company in one hundred years.

You *will* exit in your future. This is why I really think it's important that you, as the founder, frame your thoughts around exiting from the very start.

I like to teach founders and entrepreneurs that they will actually have five exits, or evolutions, in any company they are involved with. In this book I will coach you through all five exits so that you are ready for each one, and so both you and your company are prepared for future growth and stability. Let's discuss each of these exits.

## THE 5 EXITS OF AN ENTREPRENEUR

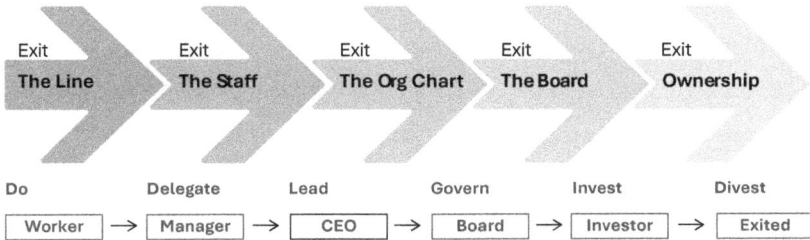

| Exit | Exit | Exit | Exit | Exit |
|------|------|------|------|------|
| **The Line** | **The Staff** | **The Org Chart** | **The Board** | **Ownership** |

| Do | Delegate | Lead | Govern | Invest | Divest |
|----|----------|------|--------|--------|--------|
| Worker → | Manager → | CEO → | Board → | Investor → | Exited |

# Exit One: Exit the Line

Every single founder starts off as a worker. Sure, you founded the business, but in the beginning, you're the person with the idea, with the knowledge, with the product. Your first months (or more likely years) were spent working *in* the business. You served the customers. You created the product. You did the selling. You handled the marketing. You were a technician or a worker at that level.

Your first exit, then, is to exit the line. It's to stop doing the day-to-day work *in* the business, so that you can start working on the business. In his book *The E-Myth Revisited*, Michael Gerber describes it very well. He explains that founders generally start off doing everything in the business, and only when they start delegating (read: exiting the line) does the business really grow into a valuable entity. (By the way, *The E-Myth Revisited* is the first of many books I will recommend in *Exit-Ready*. You should definitely read it.)[2]

---

2 Michael E. Gerber, *The E-Myth Revisited: Why Most Small Businesses Don't Work and What to Do About It* (New York: HarperBusiness, 1995), 31–42 (Entrepreneur/Manager/Technician); 116–30 ("work on" vs. "in" the business); 195–204 (organizational strategy/delegation).

*Only when founders start delegating does a business truly grow into a valuable enterprise.*

When you exit the line, you move from being the person who's actually doing everything and wearing all the hats to becoming a manager. You obtain the power to delegate. You no longer spend your days mired in the tasks it takes to run the business, and instead move into an oversight role where you spend time managing others as they complete those tasks. Think of this first exit as going from *doing* to *delegating*.

## Exit Two: Exit the Staff

As manager, you're now focused on building systems. You're figuring out what production needs to do to create better, more valuable products. And what marketing needs to do to get leads. And what sales needs to do to drive sales. And how your entire team can work together to deliver value to your customers, which is really what running a business is all about.

You're still caught in the weeds of the business, which is a good thing to start, but once those systems are in place and the business is running like a well-oiled machine, it's time to think about moving from being a manager of people to being the leader of the entire company.

During this exit, you move from manager to CEO. I recognize that for most founders, this is a symbolic or mental shift. Most of you were CEO from day one. But the mental shift is an important one to make. Many founders essentially call themselves the head chef, but they're still doing the dishes. They're still down in the weeds of the business, with their hands in the everyday tasks required to get work done.

That's really not the function of a CEO. The chief executive's role is to support and lead the officers (or other leaders: VPs, department heads, in some cases managers) of the company that are responsible for executing the vision of the board. The CEO sits between the board of directors and the people that manage the day-to-day tasks. A manager is only concerned about their department and the people that report directly to them, but the CEO is concerned with managing the managers, and ensuring that the managers and their teams are able to complete the work necessary to meet the organization's objectives.

Being a CEO requires leadership, of course, but it also requires the ability to listen to what the board wants. It requires the ability to grasp the strategic vision that the board wants executed; to communicate that vision to the officers (or others) who are leading the others on your staff; and then to oversee those teams as they execute.

Exiting the staff is a significant mental shift as you change your focus from management to leadership. I like to think of this as moving from *delegating* to *leading*.

You may have made exits one and two long ago. As businesses grow, founders are likely to make those first two exits out of necessity. But not everyone does, or they don't do so completely. So it's important to ask yourself at this point: Have I *fully* exited the line? Have I *fully* exited the staff? Or are there things I'm still holding on to? The time to make those exits complete is now. In order to be Exit-Ready you must fully exit the line and the staff.

## Exit Three: Exit the Org Chart

Exiting the org chart is when things really start to get fun for founders. I know it feels a bit daunting. After all, you're essentially writing yourself out of a job. But trust me: Exiting the org chart is essential to your freedom and to your ultimate ability to scale as an investor. You go from being bogged down by the business to scaling with the business. (And if you have or want to have multiple businesses, you cannot be on the organizational chart of all of them.)

Exiting the org chart is the exit you should aspire to from day one.

When you're in the CEO role, you manage the directors of your different departments and are ultimately responsible for ensuring that they succeed. When you exit that role and move to the board of directors, you stop being responsible for the day-to-day success of your teams and become responsible for the company's overall vision and direction. You move from *leadership* to *governance*.

Governance is important. It means ensuring that the company is held accountable to their objectives, and that the CEO in particular is held accountable to the board to execute the vision.

When you exit the org chart, you shift from being responsible for objectives and instead become responsible for the strategic vision of the company.

As you exit the org chart, you no longer have direct reports. You no longer lead the company day-to-day. Instead, you act as a strategic advisor and create the vision for the CEO to work with. You'll be communicating and working with the CEO, but not really telling the people at the company what they're going to do.

*Exiting the org chart is freedom!*

Exiting the org chart is freedom. You are still generally invested in the company as the founder, investor, or as the person who acquired

the business and worked your way through some of these exits, but you have the freedom to focus on the big picture instead of the details.

You may decide to remain as CEO of your business to be in charge of its leadership and strategic vision, but remember that if you do this you will likely be asked to stay on for some time after a sale of the business to ensure a smooth transition to the new ownership. If this does not sound like something you'd like to do, then you will want to replace yourself as CEO at least six months to a year prior to selling.

## Exit Four: Exit the Board

The next exit is to actually exit the board of directors.

Before I go further, I want to make sure to say that, as with the CEO role, not all founders choose to exit the board. Some want to keep their hands in the strategic oversight. And that can be a viable option. You don't have to go through all five exits of an entrepreneur to exit the company.

If and when you do decide to exit the board, you move from *governance* to *investment*. You stop working on the board or over the company's vision or objectives. You stop having regular contact with the CEO and officers of the company. Instead, you become a passive investor who put capital into the company, but has no governance role. When you exit the board, you're probably still going to have some conversations with the board as an investor because you want to be sure things are going right with your investment, but you won't be responsible for executing or overseeing any work.

This is a big exit. It essentially means letting go of the business you've been working in, on, and over for years if not decades.

You may never be ready to exit the board, or you may be champing at the bit to do it right away. Regardless, it's a choice you have as a founder and one you should always keep in the back of your mind.

## Exit Five: Exit the Company

The final exit is to exit from the company. This is when you move from investor to…nothing. Well, nothing except a big pile of cash in your bank account after the sale of the business.

This is the final exit from your company. You sell it, no strings attached, and walk away. Ideally, you retire to a nice beach and never think of it again. This is the ultimate goal for many founders—to have a final (successful) exit from their company and pass ownership and control on to someone else.

Other founders may not ever get to this exit—they may stay on the board of directors or continue investing in the company for their entire lives, or pass the business down to family members. But since Exit Five is what many founders consider the "ultimate" exit, we'll be talking quite a bit about it throughout this book. Likewise, even if you're not sure if you will ever want to exit your company completely, it is worth your time and effort to at least ensure that it's an option.

When you exit the company, you realize the many years you poured into the business, and you yield dividends for them. This income will set the stage for the rest of your life, and the blood, sweat, and tears you poured into the company will be returned to you.

You almost certainly aren't ready to exit your company now—financially, emotionally, or business-wise—but you should be working toward that exit. That's what this book is all about.

## When Should You Exit the Company?

"My biggest fear," my business partner said to me, "is showing up and walking out on stage and there is no one there."

We owned a large business event that attracted thousands of attendees every year and that also cost millions of dollars to produce. His

recurring nightmare, and I do mean *literally* a recurring nightmare, was that we would spend the millions of dollars to put on the event and no one would buy a ticket. The cavernous space would be empty.

Four primary owners of the company owned this event, and three of us wanted to keep doing it forever, but my one partner's fears ultimately caused us to look seriously at selling when a company owned by the large private equity firm Blackstone came calling and wanting to buy it.

Our argument to my reticent partner was to look at how well the event was doing and how much it was growing. Why sell now when we could just enjoy perpetual growth like we had for the ten years before? But our partner was adamant, so we went through the selling process, and we ultimately sold the business for the highest multiple the company had ever paid for an event. It was a huge financial win for all of us.

Interestingly enough, that sale closed in 2018, and we had a significant earnout that we successfully received 100 percent of in 2019 while we were still operating the event. At that point, operational control and management shifted over to the buyer, and we stepped back from those roles.

Then came the Covid-19 pandemic. Literally one and a half weeks before the 2020 event was to take place, the entire world shut down and all events were canceled. If we had not sold the business, we would have been looking down the barrel of a multimillion-dollar loss. We would have shown up, and no one would have been there: the realization of my partner's recurring nightmare, finally come true.

Fortunately, that did not happen because we sold the event and pocketed our earnout. The company that bought the business from us owned many events and ultimately lost, as best we can tell, over $500 million from event shutdowns due to the pandemic.

Sadly, the event that we sold never really recovered from the pandemic. It was ultimately mothballed by the buyer along with about fifty other large events they had purchased.

Was it smart to sell?

Absolutely.

Did any of us see that coming?

Arguably my nightmare-shaken partner, but really what happened with the pandemic was beyond even his most pessimistic expectations.

When you're working on the inside and you can see what's going on with the business, the right times for exiting the line, the staff, the org

chart, and even the board usually become apparent. But knowing when to exit the company—when to sell—is much harder.

The simple answer is that you should sell when either of two conditions are met: when the company can get you the amount that you want every month from investing your post-exit proceeds; or, when you realize the valuation is never going to reach that number, and you've built the company up as far as it can take you. If the latter, you exit and use those proceeds to buy another company, and then let that company get you to your ultimate destination.

*"The key is to know your number."*

The key is to know your number. That's really, really important. Otherwise, you're just guessing about whether the amount is right, or guessing about where you need to be.

Once you know your number, you go into exit planning. Your entire focus can be on how to hit your number.

One major factor that often impacts founders on the way to becoming Exit-Ready is if they have an *owner-operated business*. In these cases, the owner is essential to the business. If the founder doesn't show up for three or six months, the business is going to start to fail or at least underperform. Without the owner-operator there, the business will not and cannot continue to perform.

The opposite of an owner-operated business is a *professionally managed business*. In this type, the owner could leave the business for a year or longer and the business would grow and do just fine. Is this because the owner isn't important to the business? Of course not! It means the founder has done a good job of replacing himself or herself. If you have a professionally managed business, you have people in place who can and will run it for you. It's not going to drop in value. It's not going to tank. These founders have successfully exited the org chart.

Working in an owner-operated business does not mean you can't exit.

Many owner-operators do exit—they retire or sell or close up the business. But the profits and proceeds will be different.

If you're hoping for a bigger number—and that the business can continue to grow even after you leave—then you have to start replacing yourself. In this scenario, as you get ready to leave an Exit-Ready business, it will likely go up in value. This is partially because managers can manage better than we founders can, and partially because a well-managed business is a well-oiled machine that can't help but scale.

*If you want help actually replacing yourself, I walk through it step by step in The 7 Levels of Scale. You'll find that and a bundle of supporting tools at: https://Scalable.co/ExitReadyResources.*

## Becoming Exit-Focused to Be Exit-Ready

This chapter has given you an overview of the five exits of an entrepreneur. All (or most) are essential as your business scales, and all play an important role in the company's growth and development. As we said at the beginning of this chapter, just because you've read the last page of a book doesn't mean you understand the story the characters went through to get to that ending. And just because you previously exited a business does not mean you did it correctly or in the way that netted you the greatest amount of money at closing. The five exits we've discussed are an outline of the process that will get you to the last page of your story with your company.

This book is about helping you scale through all five exits, but ultimately, it's about making sure that you and your business are ready for you to exit the company.

To sell.

To deposit a big, fat check into your bank account and move on to the next big thing (or the next balmy beach).

And to make all that investment and time you've put into your business pay dividends for you.

CHAPTER *2*

# UNDERSTANDING YOUR NUMBER

An acquaintance of mine—we'll call him Chris—owned and led an e-commerce store for almost fifteen years. Three years ago, Chris started considering an exit. His business was owner-operated, which meant that he was spending upwards of eighty hours a week managing the staff, the marketing, and the sales team. He was burned out and ready to move on to new things.

Additionally, Chris's kids had recently graduated high school and were all in college. He was hoping to prepare for his retirement, not to mention pay for university bills and what he hoped was an upcoming wedding for his daughter.

Chris had a lot of things going for him: His business ran smoothly and was growing year over year by about 10 percent. He also had a great team in place and was in an industry that was doing well. On top of his business readiness, he was emotionally ready to exit. He felt primed to try new things and wasn't feeling a need to hold on or maintain control.

So Chris exited. Just like that. An interested buyer made a nice, seven-figure offer and he accepted. Money exchanged hands and Chris's bank account got a huge boost. His company changed leadership. It continued to grow.

Fast forward three years. Chris paid off his mortgage. He paid for tuition. He paid for a wedding. And…he ran out of money.

It wasn't that he didn't get a big payday for his company—he did—but he exited when he wasn't Exit-Ready. He exited as an owner-operator (we'll get more into that in the coming chapters), so his exit multiple was much smaller than it could have been (we'll also get into that). Additionally, Chris didn't know his number when he exited, so he took the first offer he received. While it was a lot of cash, it wasn't enough to sustain him for as long as he needed.

This is why it's important for founders to figure out their number before even considering an exit.

I'm not one to say "I told you so," but it would have taken less than a year to install professional management (we'll get into that as well) to ensure a higher exit multiple. Had Chris known his number, he could have worked to make sure he got what he needed from his company. If you know your number ahead of time, you can work to ensure that you hit that number so you get what you need out of your company, and you also avoid the risk of selling for too little or exiting too soon.

That's what this chapter is all about. What will make it worthwhile for you to actually sell your investment in the company?

As a founder, you almost certainly have an idea of what your *business* needs for you to exit. You understand what roles you play, and what will need to be done to replace you. You also may be starting to understand your emotional readiness, and as you go through the Exit-Ready process, you'll have opportunities to gauge your own emotional readiness. As Chris's story demonstrates, business readiness and emotional readiness are important, but perhaps the most important and often overlooked factor is financial readiness.

What do you want to receive financially when you exit? A million? Ten million? One hundred million? It's easy to throw out big numbers, but knowing your financial readiness is much bigger than just thinking of a number you want to get. Ideally, you're going to exit your company and sell it for a whole lot of money. But how much? Big dollar figures look really nice, but a common mistake for founders is to do like Chris did: sell their company and get a seemingly huge payday without understanding what they truly need.

To be Exit-Ready, I recommend that founders first decide and get really clear on what their number is, and then reverse engineer the growth

path for the business's revenue and profits to make sure they get to that number. On the coming pages, I'll help you to figure out the first part of that. Then the rest of this book will help you know how to reverse engineer your exit so that you get the amount you need when you leave.

Part of the Exit-Ready process is understanding the value that is locked up in your current business and finding ways to unlock that value before you sell. There are countless stories of entrepreneurs—like Chris—who sold their businesses too soon, without fully understanding how much they were worth.

For example, take Planet Fitness. TSG Consumer Partners purchased a majority stake in Planet Fitness for $35 million, and three years later the company went public at a valuation of $1.5 billion.

Roy Raymond sold Victoria's Secret to Les Wexner for $1 million in 1982. Wexner rebranded and expanded the business, which grew to $7 billion in annual sales at its peak, before selling his majority stake in 2021 for some $2 billion.[1]

---

1 Lisette Voytko, "Les Wexner Sells Majority of Stake in Victoria's Secret Parent L Brands for Some $2 Billion," *Forbes*, July 16, 2021.

Meineke Car Care was sold for $20 million, then expanded and taken public at a valuation of $3.6 billion.

I could on, but without question, not understanding valuation strategy can cost you dearly when you exit. One company that I recently worked with and had an ownership interest in was offered a 6x multiple to be acquired. During due diligence (a part of the process we'll discuss more in later chapters), I was able to unearth that the acquiring company had just received a valuation at an 11.4x multiple. Had we sold without further investigation, they would have acquired our company at 6x and then immediately earned the 5.4x additional multiple as our company was brought into theirs with the higher valuation. That would have been a mistake of about $150 million had we moved forward with the deal. It definitely pays to understand this game at the deepest level possible.

> *"What will make it worth it for you to actually sell your investment in the company?"*

## What You Need From Your Business

Here's the big, important thing that some founders fail to realize: Once you sell your company, you won't be earning money from that company anymore.

I know that's an annoyingly obvious thing to say, but you would be surprised how often this is overlooked. So I'll be super clear. Once you sell:

You aren't able to take a salary from that company anymore.

You don't receive dividends on profits.

You can't write business expenses off of your taxes.

You lose access to business perks like a company car or paid lunches.

Once you exit, you most likely won't be getting any money from your company. Instead, you'll have a big lump sum in the bank. This is great! But you can't use that money to pay your living expenses—because, in that case, it will disappear really, really quickly.

Instead, the wise thing to do would be to live off of the proceeds from *investing* that lump sum.

Best-case scenario, if you net one million dollars from your exit, that sum sits untouched. Well, not exactly; it is invested, and the money you need to live on comes from the proceeds of that investment.

I understand that there are a lot of nuances, and sometimes your company just isn't worth enough to make that happen. Regardless, part of being Exit-Ready is knowing what you need to make on the sale so you

can live off of those investments, and then reverse engineering your exit to make that happen.

Sometimes, that engineering will show you that you're not ready to exit. For example, you may realize you need to grow your business by 20 percent before you can exit. Or you'll discover that you should maintain a stake in the company so you can continue drawing some income from it. Or maybe you'll realize that with a few simple tweaks, you can get to the number you need.

Whatever it is, it starts with knowing your number.

## Calculating Your Number

To start, figure out how much money you need every month after you've sold the company. As I said earlier, after you exit, you're no longer going to be paid by the company in any capacity. So to exit successfully, you need to, at the very least, replace that monthly income, and, if possible, exceed it.

Calculating the number is easy. Start by figuring out the income you need each month and multiply it by twelve to get your desired annual income. For example, if you need to bring in $10,000 per month to replace your income, then you need $120,000 per year. Easy math, right? It gets harder, so hang with me.

Once you have your desired annual number, divide it by the estimated return on your post-exit investments. What does that mean? Well, assuming you're not planning to store cash underneath your mattress, you will need to invest the money you make from your exit. Take the amount you think you're going to make on those investments and use it to divide your desired annual number.

Important note here: Oftentimes founders assume that if they have a lot of money in the bank, they can just make a monthly withdrawal and have all the money they need. This is a huge mistake. I always recommend that founders maintain your expected income to match your current salary through investing your post-exit proceeds.

Basically, if you put all of the proceeds from your sale into the bank, and then live off of your interest on that investment, you'll be set for life with a nice nest egg. You will have income in the form of interest, and money in the bank that is growing (or at least not shrinking). You want to be able to invest that pile of money in ways you are comfortable with, that will at least equal or exceed the amount of money the company is paying you right now.

So, what you need to do is figure out exactly how much money that amount in the bank needs to be.

One word of warning: Don't be too aggressive with your estimated return, because if you think you're going to earn 25 percent a year or more on your investments, you're setting yourself up for a lot of disappointment. It might go without saying, but investments typically don't generate that much. I recommend picking something very conservative, like 5 percent or 4 percent. Doing so will give you a good picture of what to expect, and if you have some up years and down years, it will all balance out and you'll still get what you need.

Back to the calculations. The formula is this: Your desired monthly income times twelve, divided by the post-exit return that you think you're going to get on those investments, equals the minimum amount you need to sell the company for to hit your target.

Let's keep the example from above going and do some calculations so we can see this process in action. Say you need $10,000 a month in income. Multiply $10,000 times twelve months, and your investments need to earn $120,000 a year.

Assume a 5 percent average return on investment, that means we're going to need to sell this company for $2.4 million. If we get $2.4

million and we're earning 5 percent on that, it's $120,000 a year, or $10,000 a month in income, from that investment. Oh, and don't forget about taxes. You have to pay those too. So figure them into your calculations to arrive at a net cash flow number that you can live off of comfortably.

*$10,000/month x 12 [$120,000] ÷ Estimated % Return On Post-Exit Investment [5%] = $2.4 Million*

Let's try another scenario. If you know you will need $25,000 a month to pay for all of your expenses, then multiply that by twelve months to arrive at

$300,000.

Assuming a 5 percent return on investment, you will need $6 million upon exit to expect a return of $300,000 a year, and again, remember that is before taxes.

The math is easy, but as with all numbers, there is always some nuance.

For example, let's say you have a $500,000 mortgage on your house and you pay $3,000 a month. If you paid that mortgage off the top of the proceeds of your exit, you would lose some of your lump sum, but you would also lose a very expensive monthly payment. You'll need to do the math and figure out which is more advantageous for you—to pay off the mortgage first, or to start with the highest possible lump sum in the bank. The answer may be different from person to person.

**WORKSHEET – WHAT'S YOUR NUMBER?**

Desired Monthly Income:

[× 12] [Yearly Amount]  =

Estimated [%] Return On Post-Exit Investments:  [%]

Post-Exit Assets Needed:  =

Another example of nuance is business expenses. Let's say you have always had a company car. On top of that, you've had client lunches three times a week for your entire career. Maybe your company has paid for your travel to business events, but then you've tacked on family vacations. You'll need to factor in these additional expenses to your desired monthly income.

You may even be in a situation where you can't invest your proceeds immediately, and to get that return you need, you have to start another company or invest in something you think is going to appreciate significantly. This can happen when there is a significant hold back of funds in escrow to cover potential liabilities and expenses after the closing, or if you have agreed to seller financing or an earnout or other deferred payments from the sale, or where you have accepted part of the sales proceeds in the form of a rollover (investment in the new company that bought your old company). You need to be careful to base your investment income estimate on what you will actually receive in net after-tax cash at the closing, not the gross sales price.

Whatever your personal situation is, it's important to be aware of the nuances in your finances. Think about what life after the exit will look like. You don't want to go from making $10 million a year to having no income and no ability to earn it—unless you have your post-exit income needs and projected investment income mapped out.

Part of determining your number is figuring out how to go deep and get detailed with the numbers so you can work toward your exit number.

## Getting Granular with the Numbers

Getting super granular with the numbers will help you fully understand what being Exit-Ready means.

For example, let's say a woman named Sarah sells her software as a service (SaaS) company for $3 million.

Before she exited, Sarah was taking a salary of $500,000 a year.

Now she has $3 million ready to be deposited. Of course, first she has to pay taxes on her gains. Assuming a 20 percent tax rate, Sarah's $3 million is now $2.4 million. If Sarah invests that $2.4 million, she can expect a 5 percent return, meaning she will get $120,000 a year from that investment.

Sarah's previous salary was $500,000. Now it's $120,000. That's a $380,000 difference per year.

Now, it could be that Sarah wasn't really living on $500,000. Maybe she lives in a modest house and has spent about $120,000 a year on bills while investing the remaining salary. If so, Sarah is fine. But if she was living on that $500,000 and needed the same amount to continue, Sarah is going to have to cut back quite a bit.

She will have to cut back even more, though, because Sarah forgot that she used to have childcare for her four children paid for by the company. The company also paid for her cellphone and her car lease, and she ran her family travel and several meals per week through the company as well. Those combined expenses total about $5,000 per

month, or $60,000 per year, and not only are they no longer paid by the company, but they are not deductible, so they will be after-tax personal expenses post-sale. If Sarah continued to pay those expenses, it would cut her $120,000 cash flow in half, to just $60,000.

The bottom line here is that Sarah needs quite a bit more than $3 million from her exit to maintain her current standard of living.

How does Sarah know when it's time to sell? Well, she darn sure shouldn't sell before she's maximized the value of her company in relation to the amount of money she wants to be able to live off after she sells. That's what being Exit-Ready is all about.

## It's Not Just About Profits

Before I move on to talk about multiples and levels of risk in getting Exit-Ready, I want to be really clear on one thing: The sales price of a business isn't just about profits.

You would think that if you needed a certain number out of a company, then you would just need to increase sales and therefore profits to a point where the sales price would increase. That makes sense when it comes to lemonade stands, but your business isn't child's play.

If you've been in business for a while, you know that it's not terribly hard to go from $50,000 to $100,000, and even from $50,000 to $500,000. Good business owners can do that over and over. Once you know business and you implement strategies to increase valuation and increase profitability, you can probably raise your profits in a matter of a few quarters.

Part of the purpose of this book is helping you to increase your profits so that you can sell your business for the maximum price, but there is so much more to the sales price than that. There are so many factors—and the number you get is going to vary widely depending on sales multiple, transferable value, industry, level of risk, and much more.

Here are a couple of points for clarity. Businesses typically sell for a multiple of their profits. This is referred to as the "sales multiple." It sounds like it should be called the "profit multiple" because it is literally a multiple of the profits, but what it provides is the sale price for the business, so we refer to it as the sales multiple.

We have discussed transferable value at some length, but it is also important to understand that businesses in different industries typically carry different levels of transferable value and sell at different multiples. If your business is in a highly risky industry like fireworks manufacturing (risky for many reasons, from safety to regulations to product liability), the sales multiple is likely to be significantly less than if your business is in a popular, trendy, low-risk industry like, say, SaaS.

Your number will never be a linear application. There is no hard-and-fast formula that says profits times multiple equals sales price. Instead, there are all kinds of things you can do to increase your sales price, from retooling the management team, to shifting your industry, to changing your operating strategies or business model.

And if you want to hit your number, you'll probably need a little bit of strategy to do so. Stay tuned for that.

## Let's Get Exit-Ready

Oftentimes panic sets in after a founder has figured out their number. They see this huge cash amount that they need to live on, and they start to wonder if they will ever exit.

Let me reassure you: That number is not impossible.

How do I know when I don't necessarily know you or your business? I know you've been living off the business since you founded it. I know you've been getting money out of the business to pay your

living expenses, so I know the business has some value. I know it has enough value to have sustained you so far.

But I also know that it's easy to make mistakes on exit, and that small tweaks can make a huge difference. That's why I wrote this book: I want to help founders not to make the mistakes that Chris and so many others have made.

On the coming pages, I'll teach you about transferable value, multiples, and about how to reverse engineer your business so that you can hit your number and live the life you want. I'll share little-known tricks on how businesses can increase their sales price and profit on exit, and how you can make sure you have all the tools in your toolbox to make it happen.

A lot of it comes down to the quality of earnings we can build in the company that we've got, and how can we take advantage of several tools and tricks that increase your transferable value.

Before we move on, though, I want to make sure to point out that there are lots of reasons to exit. You might see a downturn coming. You might be retiring or relocating. Maybe you went through a divorce, or you have challenges with partners. Maybe there's just a shiny object that you want to pursue. There's nothing wrong with any of those reasons. If you want to sell before you are Exit-Ready, that's your prerogative.

*"There are a lot of reasons to exit."*

But, as we've already seen, a lot of people are really surprised when they sell their business and then the money goes away. Even though they've got this big pile of money, it disappears really quickly. I want you to have all of the information you need so that you can sell on your timing, and get the most possible from your company.

A bit later I'll take you through the process of reverse engineering your target so that you can manage growth toward that target. Peter Drucker famously said, "What gets measured gets managed." I've found this to prove true, especially when it comes to founders trying to manage their companies toward an exit. But first, we have to talk about multiples.

CHAPTER 3

# UNDERSTANDING MULTIPLES

There we were, sitting face-to-face, at a Denny's no less. It was just me and the seller of a business that I was in the process of buying. The originally proposed valuation from the seller was $20 million, but everything I could find on valuations for similar businesses told me that this business was only worth about $3 million as it stood.

So we had agreed to meet over breakfast to hash out a valuation for me to purchase my interest in the business. The seller explained how they had come up with $20 million. There was no science. It was just what they thought the business should be worth, approximately one times sales.

The challenge, I explained, was that businesses like theirs sold for a multiple of revenue, not sales, and that the multiple for an owner-operated publishing business like theirs was typically somewhere between two times and three times profit. We talked more. I showed him some data from charts that are published by a business-valuation company. We ultimately agreed that the valuation should be $3 million.

It was a fair price for where the business was at the time that I bought into it, but I saw the potential for much, much more. The business had three distinct components and no professional management. I knew that if we separated the business into those three components, it could instantly be worth more, because the multiple for a publishing business was so much lower than the multiples for the other two types of businesses embedded within the publishing business.

After closing, we installed professional management and broke the one company into three. After that, the original component was worth five times profits, but the other two were worth 10 times and 11.5 times, respectively. That took the overall valuation from $3 million to about $8.3 million, and that was without any additional growth. We later realized that there were even more sub-businesses within the core company, and to date we have exited five different companies from the one and still generate eight figures from the remaining business!

I was able to acquire the business at a far lower price than the seller wanted because I understood multiples and the seller did not. Then, I was able to divide and sell parts of the company that I had purchased for significantly more than I paid for the whole thing because I understood multiple arbitrage— basically, how to reposition the company, or parts of it, to be able to apply a higher multiple than the company could command prior to that repositioning.

Bottom line, here's what you need to know: Most businesses sell for a multiple of their profits.

When someone buys a company, they buy it in hopes of future income. They're investing in what they can earn, and so generally it is bought for a portion of the income that they can expect to receive. For example, if a company is profiting $1 million every year, it will likely sell at some multiple of $1 million.

In light of that, an owner can expect to receive several years' worth of profitability when they exit.

What that multiple is…depends—and it can vary greatly.

That's what we're going to talk about in this chapter: the types of profits that companies make, and then how multiples are calculated and applied based on those profits.

## The Types of Profits

Profit is profit, right?

Well, yes and no. At the very basic level, incoming money, minus expenses, equals profit. But because your business is unique and complex, as are all other businesses, profits can take on many definitions. Because multiples are decided by profits, it is helpful to discuss different types of profit. When it comes to multiples, the profit type is usually determined by the type of business you have. Below I'll explain the types of profit and how they are calculated, and then we'll discuss how these types play into multiples.

The goal is to find the actual *operating profit* of the company. You need to know what the business's profit must be to get to your desired "number" (sales price) on exit. You want to make sure that you are careful and accurate with your calculations—that real expenses are taken out, and that fictitious expenses (like depreciation and amortization) are accounted for. I recommend that you seek the advice of your accounting and tax professionals as you go through this process.

## Type One: Profit as "SDE"

If your business is owner-operated (i.e., you're the owner and CEO or you are critical to the operations), then you will likely use a profit type called *seller discretionary earnings,* or SDE. This means that the profits include everything the business makes in profit, plus any extra salary or compensation that you pay yourself, plus any owner benefits.

For example, if you pay yourself a salary of $500,000, and you write off a retreat trip to Europe, and you have a company car, then all that money would be added together with the company's profits to get the SDE.

SDE profits can be pretty complex—lots of personal expenses for the owner are often paid for by a company. Maybe your Tesla is on the books, or perhaps your babysitter or cable bill or other household expenses. Maybe you put your spouse or even your older kids on the

payroll so they effectively have an allowance. These are all perfectly reasonable and acceptable things that owners do to write off expenses, and the items will all be added back to profits toward the SDE.

## Type Two: Profit as "EBITDA"

If your business is professionally managed—i.e., you are no longer an owner-operator—we use a different profit type when figuring multiples. Professionally managed businesses use a type called EBITDA, which stands for *earnings before interest, taxes, depreciation*, and *amortization*. The reason interest, taxes, depreciation, and amortization are taken out of the profits is because they aren't actually operating expenses.

Interest is usually related to debt that was either used to acquire capital assets for the company or to acquire the company itself. Interest is not an expense for determining operating profit. Taxes are based on profits, but they aren't profits in and of themselves, nor are they necessary to operate the company, so to know what our true profits are, both interest expense and tax expenses need to be taken out.

Depreciation is a fictitious expense that accountants deduct based on the useful life of a given asset, and thus is not an expense necessary to the operation of the business. If your company buys an asset that can be used in the business over a number of years before you have to buy another one, the tax code allows you to write it off over the period of its useful life.

For example, imagine purchasing a million-dollar asset with a ten-year useful life and then writing off $100,000 a year. You are not actually spending the $100,000, but for accounting purposes you acknowledge in the financial statements that you have used up about one-tenth of the total useful life of the asset, meaning you write off a tenth of the purchase price (which is $100,000) each year.

You spent the actual $1 million when you bought the asset, and you won't spend any money to buy another one until the original needs to be replaced. There is no actual cash out of pocket happening as a result of the write-off. Therefore, we ignore depreciation for determining EBITDA.

Amortization is similar, except that depreciation applies to physical assets while amortization applies to intangibles like intellectual property—say, if you bought a copyright or a patent or a brand or something like that, it is amortized over its usable life.

## Type Three: Profits as Recurring Revenue Based

Subscription businesses are companies that have recurring revenue. This includes many SaaS companies and also others that have an auto-ship or a subscription box service. If the revenue can be measured on a consistent basis—say, monthly or quarterly—and people are paying the bill over and over, then that's a subscription business. I want to be really clear that this is not an installment company. If you're selling a high-priced item (say, a coaching service) and people are allowed to pay in installments (maybe $10,000 per quarter for two years) that's not a subscription. After two years, the revenue stops as the product is paid for.

> *"ARR is the holy grail because you can get a multiple of the revenue that's recurring, not a multiple of profit."*

A company with *annual recurring revenue* (ARR) is the holy grail—because you can get a multiple of the revenue that's recurring, not a multiple of profit. These are the types of companies that people want to acquire most—and often fetch the highest multiples because revenue is recurring and automatically comes in, regardless of sales cycles and other factors.

## Calculating Multiples

For almost all businesses other than true subscription companies, we will use a multiple of SDE or EBITDA, so I'll address ARR businesses in a different section.

Once the profit has been calculated—either by SDE or EBITDA—that profit is multiplied by what we call an exit multiple or sales multiple.

They both mean the same thing for our purposes. The big question is: Which exit multiple should we use? After all, a multiple of 2.5 and 10 create very different sales prices for determining valuation.

I'm sure it comes as no surprise that exit multiples are not standard or consistent across the board—which is a good thing. After all, when you've put a lifetime of blood, sweat, and tears into a business, the last thing you want to do is pigeonhole it into a simple formula that fails to consider important specifics.

In the simplest terms, multiples are calculated based on what other businesses in that niche are selling for. We call these *comps* or *comparables* because we are comparing the business that we are valuing to similar businesses and what they sold for. The more similar the previously sold "comp" is to the business we are now trying to value, the more accurate the multiple is likely to be.

The company's industry is a significant factor, too, because different industries have different profit margins, are more/less desirable or in demand to investors at any given time, have varying risk profiles, or may be experiencing unique boons or challenges. Therefore, different industries have different multiples.

In addition, a business's multiple depends on the type of company it is (the entity structure—partnership, LLC, corporation, etc.), revenue size, geographic location, and a variety of other factors.

To get the average number that similar businesses are selling for, we use what is called a *comp cohort*. A comp cohort is a group of comparable businesses in the same niche that have recently sold. In order to calculate a multiple, we look at what each business in the cohort sold for and then divide that total aggregated selling price by the number of businesses that sold. That tells us what the multiple of profit was.

| COHORT METHOD | | EXAMPLE |
|---|---|---|
| Aggregate sales of all businesses sold in the same niche | | $25,000,000 |
| # of businesses sold: ÷ | | ÷ 25 Businesses |
| Cohort sales amount: = | | = $1,000,000 |
| Company profit: ÷ | | ÷ $250,000 Profit |
| Multiplier: = | | = × 4 Multiplier |

For example, if there are twenty-five businesses in the cohort and the sale price of all twenty-five businesses totaled $25 million, then the cohort sales number is $1 million each. If a company has profits of $250,000, then their multiplier is $1 million divided by $250,000, which means the multiplier is 4. That's a quick, simplified explanation, but it's important to at least have a basic understanding of how profits and multiples work as you work toward being Exit-Ready.

In the next section I'm going to give you some general guidelines about how multiples are determined, as well as some charts and other resources you can use to help figure out your number. Remember that multiples vary. If someone tells you that your company is going to sell for a multiple of 5, you probably should take that with a huge grain of salt, because it's almost always a range.

With that said, any guidelines *I* give you should also be taken with a grain of salt and used just for initial planning. You should always work with a good acquisitions advisor and get the legal counsel you need to ensure the maximum price for your business.

## Roland's Favorite Resources for Calculating Multiples

### 1. New York University's Stern School of Business, pages.stern. nyu.edu

NYU's Stern School of Business publishes a chart with annual data on the multiples of profit or EBITDA that companies have actually sold for. There's no better way to calculate your company's likely sale price than to find out what comparable companies in comparable industries that are (ideally) comparable sizes have sold for. Caveat: This data, while strong, is frequently subject to adjustment up or down based on the size of your company and who the buyer is.

If you look at the data, you'll see categories for lots of different kinds of businesses, so you should be able to arrive at a baseline for your business. Unless you own a particularly specialized company (for example, you sell retrofitted safety gas caps for automobiles), you can probably find several similar businesses. Even if you own the retrofitted gas caps company, you can find companies that sell auto parts that will give you a good baseline.

My recommendation is to come up with a few categories that represent your company—for example: auto parts, auto mechanics, machine parts—and then try them all. That's going to give you a broad guideline for what your multiplier will be that you can then use to determine if you're Exit-Ready.

### 2. Equidam, equidam.com

Equidam's data is much more detailed than NYU's. It gives you many more categories, so if you can't find the data you're looking for from Stern, this is the next place I would look.

### 3. Google, google.com

You obviously know how to Google things, so it probably seems a bit trite to include the leading search engine in this list, but honestly, oftentimes the best source for initial data on multipliers is Google. Simply search "sales multiple for X type of companies," and a range should emerge. Even if the range is multiples of 4 to 10, you can at least get a basic range and see what factors are impacting those multiples.

**4. Paid Resources,** Varies

There are also many paid resources available to help you calculate multiples. Sometimes the quickest and most effective way to get what you need is to pay a pro to do it. If the categories of your business are tricky, or if you're having a hard time getting good data, I recommend finding a paid firm that can help you find your sales multiple. BVR (Business Valuation Resources) has a lot of great paid-subscription-based valuation information for a variety of businesses across multiple industries. It is well worth the subscription price if you are going to be doing valuations, acquisitions, or sales on a regular basis.

## Adjusting Multiples for the Size and Scope of the Business

One thing to remember when you are getting data from larger services (like those I've shown you in this chapter) is that they generally collect data for larger transactions. For example, when a private equity company buys a public company as a strategic buyer, they pay a lot more.

If you're a small or medium-sized company you will need to adjust the multiple numbers listed on the charts I suggested above. If you own an advertising agency that is professionally managed and generating $1 million in EBITDA, and you look up advertising agencies and see that the multiple is

16, you are not likely to be able to sell your advertising agency for $16 million (16x multiple times $1 million EBITDA/profit).

Smaller companies sell for smaller multiples, so I find a good rule of thumb is to divide the multiple from the charts by 4 to get a much better idea of what the multiple for that business will actually be.

For our advertising agency example, if the multiple on the charts

is showing 16, we would divide that by 4 to get a multiple of 4 to apply to value the advertising agency we are working with—16x per the chart divided by 4 = 4x multiple. We would then multiple the $1 million EBITDA of the agency we are valuing by the 4x multiple to get a valuation of $4 million for that business.

## Reverse Engineering Profits and Multiples

Maureen and Matthew spent more than twenty years building one of the largest ATM networks in the United States. After years of their machines doling out cash to tens of thousands of customers, they decided it was time for the business to put one big payment in their hands. They were ready to exit.

The timing was right; the industry was consolidating rapidly, and another major player in the space was on the hunt for large networks to acquire. That player approached Maureen and Matthew and made an offer, and that's when they came to me for help getting the business Exit-Ready. This included determining what price they needed to sell for to realize their post-sale income and lifestyle goals, and negotiating the sale with the company that wanted to acquire them.

I'll walk you through the process using Maureen and Matt as an example.

Once you understand how profit types and multiples work, you can reverse engineer the numbers to make sure you and your business are Exit-Ready.

Think of the number that you would like to sell your business for. I know that's a complicated question, and one that takes some thought. But as we discussed in chapter 2, it is vital to decide how much you need to get out of your business to live the life you want and have the ongoing income you need. Also, think about how much you have put into your business and what you have tied up in it.

For Maureen and Matthew, that number was $30 million. To help them determine the minimum EBITDA the business would need to be generating to permit a sale at $30 million, we just needed to divide the $30 million "number" by the exit multiple. That would tell us the minimum required EBITDA to exit at the desired valuation.

Because we had an initial offer, we were able to use the offer to see how close we would be to Maureen and Matthew's target valuation number. The offer was at a multiple of 6x (which is a common starting place for private equity firms). I find that frequently the initial range discussed is "between six and eight times EBITDA."

So in this case we divided the $30 million target valuation by the proposed offer multiple of 6 and found that the business would need to be generating a minimum EBITDA of $5 million ($30 million EBITDA divided by 6x multiple).

If we did not already have an offer, we would have determined the valuation multiple by the cohort method discussed earlier.

You can also reverse engineer your multiple. For example, if you see most companies in your industry sell for a profit multiple between 2 and 5, you can reverse engineer the math to ensure that your business possesses the qualities of the comparable businesses that sold at the highest end of the range, so that you can also sell at the high end. The multiplier generally swings based on how well you've prepared yourself to get Exit-Ready. One of the main goals of this book is to put you at the higher end of that spectrum.

We will cover much more of this in the coming chapters, but essentially, if you do this math and see that your profits are much lower than the minimum required, then you know you need some time and work to bring profits up to be Exit-Ready at your desired number. Likewise, if your profits are much higher than your minimum EBITDA (or SDE), then you can do something that everyone wants to do and raise your desired price.

**SDE OR EBITDA BASED ON EARNINGS**

**< $1 MILLION**     **$1 – 1.5 M**     **> $1.5 MILLION**

| Use | TYPE OF BUYER | Use |
|-----|---------------|-----|
| **SDE** | Individual Buyer | **EBITDA** |
| See table below: | Strategic Buyer or Private Equity Buyer | |

| SDE | Multiple | Business Value | |
|-----|----------|----------------|---|
| $50,000 | 1.0 –1.25 | $50,000 – $62,500 | |
| $75,000 | 1.1 – 1.8 | $82,500 – $135.000 | |
| $100,000 | 2.0 – 2.7 | $200,000 – $270.000 | |
| $200,000 | 2.5 – 3.0 | $500,000 – $600,000 | See: |
| $500,000 | 3.0 – 4.0 | $1,500,000 – $2,000,000 | equidam.com |
| $1,000,000 | 3.25 – 4.25 | $3,250,000 – $4,250,000 | pages.stem.nyu.edu |

## Basic Multiple Data

Here is some basic rule-of-thumb data on multiples that you can use as a reference (of course, not every industry observes these numbers, but as a general rule, they work pretty well consistently):

- Private equity sales garner higher multiples, but they generally require the business to have more than $10 million in revenue and $2 million in profit per year at a minimum. Use the charts from Stern School and Equidam to find the multiples most applicable to your business, and don't forget to divide by 4.

- Owner-operated businesses generally use an exit multiple between 2 and 3. They also must add owner expenses back into the profits. You can use the 2 to 3 range, or the chart above, or paid services like BVR. com to determine the applicable multiple for these businesses.

- The average multiple for professionally managed companies (using EBITDA) is 4.5 across all industries as of this writing.

- Companies with annual recurring revenue (ARR) can garner exit multiples in the range of 10 to 20 or more, although as of this writing they have trended more toward 7 to 10 times ARR—and the businesses must be profitable.

## Multiples in Action

I'm going to spend the next few pages giving some case studies of how profit types and multiples work. Like all examples in this book, these are modified—derived from a variety of companies that I have exited personally or helped to exit—but they should give you an idea of how exit multiples work and how companies can adjust them to maximize sales price.

**Case Study 1: Professionally Managed Business To Private Equity Buyer**

Annual EBITDA: $2 million

Multiple: 8

Anticipated Sales Price: $16 million

Brett built his online video tips site from scratch up to annual profit of $2 million on sales of $4.5 million. Like most business owners, he never thought about selling until he was approached by a private equity firm that wanted to acquire his business as a front-end lead generating channel for a video editing SaaS that the firm already owned.

Brett asked me to help him with the deal, and we determined that he needed to sell for at least $16 million to provide the roughly $800,000 per year that he needed to support his lifestyle and savings goals. Easy math told us that he would need to sell the business for a multiple of 8 to realize his goal. That number was determined by dividing the $16 million target sales valuation by the $2 million profit that the business generated. ($16 million divided by $2 million = 8x required multiple).

We entered the negotiations, which started at 5.5 times, and worked our way through several of the Exit-Ready strategies until we finally agreed on a $16 million valuation. Brett was excited, and the deal was done. Interestingly—and this does happen from time to time—the private equity firm did not have operators who possessed the same marketing and management skills as Brett, and they eventually ended up selling the business *back* to Brett (who kept all of the money from the initial sale) for 95 percent less than they bought it for. So Brett ended up keeping the money from the sale plus got the business back for pennies on the dollar.

Private equity deals are among the most frequent and largest sales transactions, and they're usually only available to companies that are profitable and well-managed. Other deals may involve strategic buyers who are either institutional, high-net-worth individuals, family offices, competitors, or owners in complementary business lines.

While I've seen private equity sales with gross sales or revenue in the single-digit millions of dollars, as a general rule, these deals are with companies that have over $10 million (Or £10 million, €10 million, depending on the local currency) in annual revenue.

The question you're probably asking is: Is it possible to do a deal smaller than that? Yes, it's possible. But to get the most for your money, my advice is that you really don't want to sell under about $10 million in sales and about $2 million in EBITDA. In an ideal world, if you're not quite there, you should hang on, double down, and get to those numbers. Then you'll get much more from your sale. If you're not quite to the $10 million in sales or $2 million in EBITDA, don't worry, there are lots of ways to get there (fairly quickly). My own firm specializes in helping businesses do just that. Check out our resources at https://Scalable.co/ExitReadyResources.

Most private equity deals I have been part of begin with an opening offer multiple range of 6 to 8. It is reasonable to expect offers in this range if your company is professionally managed and generating EBITDA in $2 million-plus territory. While this multiple is not a hard-and-fast rule, it's a good general range to expect. The interesting thing to me about Brett's deal was that he was an owner-operator. We were able to negotiate the unusually high multiple because the buyer wanted Brett's business as a strategic acquisition.

**Case Study 2: Owner-Operated Business Sold To Strategic Corporate Buyer**

Profit Value: $100,000

Multiple: 12

Anticipated Sales Price: $1.2 million

As noted in the previous example, if your company currently has gross sales under $10 million (£10 million, €10 million, depending on where you are in the world), then you're probably not quite big enough yet to sell to private equity—but it is not impossible. In these cases, it can be advantageous to look for a strategic buyer, usually another company, that could benefit from what your business has built. That might be software, systems, a team of executives, researchers or managers, a sales team, or your company's ability to generate customers a strategic buyer could want.

If you are not quite big enough for private equity but would still like a shot at a multiple higher than the 2 to 5 you might expect as an owner-operator seller, it makes sense to explore your options with strategics. Strategic buyers can be a good option before hitting private equity minimums for other reasons as well. Maybe you're ready to retire, you're moving, you have a family situation, you need to acquire another business, or you want to do something new. In those situations, your best bet is trying to find a strategic buyer.

Natalia was making money hand over fist for several years and then ran into challenges as interest rates, inflation, advertising, and housing costs all rose and the economy took a downturn. Her company

was an education business that helped aspiring yoga instructors build their own practices. At its peak, she was taking home about $4 million per year, but after waiting a bit too long to adjust the size of her staff and several unsuccessful attempts to find new ways to get customers, she was actually losing $100,000 per month when she came to me for help.

We started with an in-depth audit to identify cost-saving opportunities and stop the bleeding. We were able to quickly find about $100,000 in monthly expenses that could be trimmed immediately. That brought the business to breakeven. A few more minor adjustments wrung out another $100,000 worth of annualized profits, all without making any changes to the business model.

At that point, I faced quite a challenge because it's very difficult to sell a company that is not making much profit. And it's extremely challenging if the business make a lot of profit in the past but has been trending downward. I like a challenge, though, so I was determined to see what we could do.

I realized immediately that Natalia's business had a customer base that other companies might be very interested in. Her clients needed a software platform to run their businesses online, and there were several platforms competing for those customers.

So I reached out to three of the companies that I thought might potentially acquire Natalia's business, and all three were interested. They were not concerned about the lack of profitability because they did not want her core business. They only wanted her customers.

After initial meetings, three offers came quickly. We were ultimately able to sell Natalia's business to one of the bidders for 12 times her annual profit, with additional earnouts if the business overperformed. It was an amazing result and a very high multiple for an owner-operated business earning minimal profits on downward-trending revenue.

**Case Study 3: Owner-Operated Business To Strategic Corporate Buyer**

Profit Value: $2.4 million

Multiple: 14.2

Tori, Enrico, Nikki, and Armando were best friends who started off in real estate investing as house-flippers. They would buy properties, fix them up, and sell them. That got to be a grind pretty quickly, and they decided they could do much better keeping the houses they fixed up and renting them out. Eventually, they decided to stop the fixing and repairing and just focus on property management.

Together, each with their own special skills that complemented the others in the business, they built their property management company to an impressive $2.4 million in profits. While they heard about people in the industry selling— as private equity and major players began to gobble up smaller management companies—they had no real desire or ambition to sell.

Then, out of the blue, they received an inquiry from a larger competitor who was interested in possibly acquiring their business. They came to me to help them negotiate the deal, and we got to work. The initial offer was strong, $21 million on $2.4 million of profit, which represented a multiple of 8.75. Unfortunately, just as we got into negotiations, it was announced that pending legislation had been enacted which severely restricted several of the properties my seller was operating. That caused the potential buyer to lower their offer to $14 million. That was still decent at a 5.8 multiple, but I was determined to do better.

After quite a bit of research, I was able to dissect several previous transactions this interested company had made. (They were in triple digits for acquisitions—that's over one hundred!) I reviewed their prior deals, researched the pending legislation, analyzed and segmented revenue- and profit-generating opportunities, and ultimately negotiated an offer that was even *higher* than the original using several creative techniques, a lot of good will, and even a round of golf with the buyer's acquisition team!

In the end we sold at a 14.2 times multiple, which is unheard of given the facts of the situation.

If you're an owner-operator, you have to add back to the profits (SDE) all of the owner compensation in excess of what you have to pay a manager. Any extra salary you are paying or benefits that you get for being an owner (i.e., the things you write off) are added back in.

Let's say that you own and operate a business and pay yourself no salary. To adjust your profits to reflect SDE, you would need to determine the average cost of a manager for a business in your location and of your revenue, and then deduct that from your current profit.

You can use tools like Payscale.com and Salary.com to help you find out what a manager should cost, then deduct that amount from your profits. This accurately reflects what a buyer would have to pay someone to run the business you are leaving so they could replace you.

So if you take no salary and profits are $200,000 per year, and you research and learn that a manager who could do what you do in that business typically makes $85,000 per year, then you would reduce your $200,000 profits by $85,000, and the revised profit number you would apply the multiple to would be $115,000.

Similarly, if you overpaid yourself in cash and benefits, you would add the non-normal. non-standard amounts back to profits. So if your business made $200,000 in profits even after paying you $200,000 more than a manager would cost to do what you do in the business, plus the business paid $50,000 for a trip for your family, $25,000 in car payments for your personal vehicle, and $25,000 in meals during the year, you would add back all of that to your $200,000 profit to arrive at an SDE of $500,000 ($200,000 existing profit + $200,000 excess salary/benefits + $50,000 trip + $25,000 car + $25,000 meals = $500,000).

(With this in mind, EBITDA essentially equals SDE plus owner comp and benefits.)

*"EBITDA = SDE + owner comp & benefits"*

Multiples tend to be lower in owner-operated businesses (which is why you'll find in the coming chapters that I often encourage owners to exit the org chart before pursuing a sale). If a company has $1 million in profits, with a 2.5 multiple, it should sell for approximately $2.5 million. By installing professional management (at a cost of maybe $100,000 each year), the multiple goes up to 4.5, creating a sales price of $4.5 million. It almost doubles!

It's still going to be a million-dollar profit business, but now the profit type will be EBITDA, which means we're also going to get rid of all of the extra, nonoperational expenses that the owner was deducting.

As we saw earlier, these can add up to a lot—the owner's salary that's over a standard manager's salary, any trips that have been written off, a company car, cable and internet, the babysitter…who knows? All the things they wrote off are now added back into the profits, making the sales price much higher.

The reason professionally managed companies go for a higher multiple is because more people can invest, meaning there is lower risk. In this example, it's a $2 million swing, but for many companies it's much more than that.

One of the strategies we use a lot at EPIC and in my businesses is to acquire owner-operated businesses, install professional management, and then get a big bump in sales price. But this also provides real motivation for you to hire professional managers and replace yourself. This will get your business bumped up to a higher value and result in a whole lot more money on your exit.

## Case Study 4: Subscription Businesses

Profit Value (ARR): $1.2 million

Multiple: 10

Anticipated Sales Price: $12 million

We touched on subscription businesses earlier. The reason they are the holy grail as far as exits go is that when there is recurring revenue, you can actually get a multiple of the revenue that is recurring, not a multiple of profit. For example, let's say you developed a SaaS product that costs $25 a month. That $25 is billed every month as long as the customer is using the product. (Note: It's very important that this product is never paid off. If a company buys software and pays $100 per month for one year for a total of $1,200, then it's not recurring revenue.)

Back to the SaaS example above. Let's say you have four thousand customers who pay for your SaaS subscription. That's $100,000 in monthly recurring revenue, which adds up to $1.2 million in ARR. That $1.2 million counts directly toward your profit, so you can add that amount into other profits coming into the company to increase your profit value.

Companies with ARR can fetch some of the highest multiples I've seen. If the company has more than $1 million a year in ARR, I've seen exit multiples as high as 10 to 20 times ARR, although, as I mentioned earlier, that has fallen into the 7 to 10 range as of this writing. Even those with less than $1 million in ARR can garner an exit multiple of 3 to 10 provided they are making a profit.

This is why so many companies, even if they sell standard products or services, add subscription services into their offerings. It's a great way to add products and increase profitability and the exit multiple.

For example, we owned a business that generated content for people who own websites, newsletters, blogs, and social media accounts. Originally the company did one-off content creation on short-term contracts. As the business grew, we realized it would be worth substantially more if we switched to a subscription model. We made the change and instantly increased the multiple of the business from a 3 to 8.

## The Exit Multiple Landscape

The exit multiple landscape is obviously very fluid and changes almost daily. But I want to give you a good picture of what to expect as you get ready to exit, as demonstrated in the following examples.

### Owner-Operated Businesses

**Revenue:** $100,000–$10 million

**Profits:** $20,000–$2 million

**Approximate Multiple:** 2.5 times SDE

**Professionally Managed Businesses (Small)**

**Revenue:** Under $10 million

**Profits:** Under $2 million

**Approximate Multiple:** 4.5 times EBITDA

**Note:** This sector has shown a 19 percent year-over-year increase. Why? Because investors want to invest in professionally managed companies that are showing good, steady growth and strong profits.

**Professionally Managed Businesses (Midsized) with Private Equity Buyers**

**Revenue:** Over $10 million

**Profits:** Over $2 million

**Approximate Multiple:** 15.2 times EBITDA

**Note:** This sector has shown a 32 percent year-over-year increase for the same reason as small businesses. But notice that the multiple is almost 4 times higher than for small businesses after crossing the threshold of $10 million in revenue.

**IPO or SPAC NASDAQ PE Multiples**

**Revenue:** Over $10 million

**Profits:** Over $2 million

**Approximate Multiple:** 35 times EBITDA (just use whatever the current average Price/Earnings (P/E) ratio is for the NASDAQ composite to determine this multiple.

## The Numbers Game is Never Cut-and-Dried

I've given you a lot of numbers on the last few pages, numbers that should help you to calculate some basic data points as you start to exit. But here's the deal: There are so many dependencies in multiples that it's impossible to give cut-and-dried numbers. You can guess you might be able to garner a multiple of 4, but when you get to the table, things may change. Maybe you'll get 3, maybe you'll get 6, or maybe you'll have me help you get to 12. You just never know until you are in the thick of it and get to run all your Exit-Ready strategies.

Honestly, I love this.

I don't want things to be cut-and-dried. That's business. Part of the fun— especially for entrepreneurial types like me—is that there is no line in the sand. I can make things whatever I want to make them. I can be creative. I can tweak numbers. I can employ strategies. I can find ways to get as much money as possible out of the work I do.

As you have seen from story after story in this section, valuation takes a lot of different things into consideration—that's good, because your business is unique. You have different products, different people, different earnings, different everything. It's a game. There is no set formula, but there are lots of (entirely legal and ethical) ways to game the formula so you can get the most money possible as you exit.

You've seen that we can take a business that is generating a loss and sell it for seven figures. We can take a business that has unfavorable legislation passed in the middle of the negotiation and recover from a price drop to sell at a premium over and above the initial offer. We can sell owner-operated businesses to strategic acquirers for the same multiples usually reserved for private equity sales. Anything is possible. You just have to understand the game, know what is important to your potential buyer, and shape your company during the Exit-Ready process into the type of business that buyers will value the most.

In the coming chapters, we'll talk more about how to get to the higher end of the spectrum and how to make sure your exit multiples are the most they can be. By understanding the factors involved in sales multiples, as well as profits, you'll discover many ways to help your business sell for significantly more than it would have otherwise. You just have to be Exit-Ready.

CHAPTER $4$

# UNDERSTANDING LEVELS OF RISK

Marty, Phil, and Stu were picking out personal airplanes and contemplating Ferraris and exotic travel adventures after receiving an initial offer of just over $200 million for their business. They had built a popular and wildly profitable health supplement business and were ready to cash out and enjoy early retirement.

The private equity firm interested in acquiring their business came in with a solid opening offer and then gradually increased it during negotiations to the mouthwatering number that was now in the letter of intent. The only thing remaining was the buyer's due diligence, and that's where it all ground to a halt.

During due diligence, the buyer's attorneys found multiple marketing and sales materials that they felt did not meet applicable government compliance regarding claims and testimonials.

The solution was to change the materials to make them compliant, but the changes would eviscerate the lead flow and make acquiring customers at acceptable cost almost impossible. Ultimately, the deal died and the owners had to completely scratch all of their marketing and begin again. This time they focused on staying compliant and eliminating as much of the risk as possible to any potential buyer. You know what? They did it. They found a way to sell products in the new company in compliance at scale. They had to find a new buyer and run a new process. All of this took a couple of years, but they were able to sell the new business at close to the offer price of the old one. If you ever wanted to see a night-and-day difference in how risk impacts business salability, this is the one to dive into.

We've talked about what it means to exit.

We've talked about profits and multiples and how to maximize your sales price.

Before we get further into the Exit-Ready process, we need to do a deep dive into levels of risk.

Risk controls how much you will ultimately be able to sell your business for. Essentially, when your operation is a sure thing and has 99.99 percent steady, profitable growth, you can probably garner a higher multiple and higher price. As we saw in the last chapter, this is why companies with recurring revenue (ARR) go for higher multiples than other businesses.

On the flip side, if there is a level of risk with your business—maybe it is highly susceptible to supply and demand issues, or it ebbs and flows with markets—then your multiple will be lower.

There are many factors that impact risk, which means that like all things exit-related, the number is a bit squishy. It can vary greatly.

## Factors That Impact Risk:

1 – Industry

2 – Deal Size

3 – EBITDA or SDE size

4 – Industry Diversification

5 – Ownership and Management

In this chapter, we will examine five primary factors that impact risk and discuss strategies to minimize risk and increase your multiple.

## Risk Factor One: Industry

Different industries have different levels of risk. For example, health-related industry businesses must comply with complex and sometimes unclear HIPAA requirements. Financial companies have SEC and FinCEN (Financial Crimes Enforcement Network) compliance

requirements. Bungee-jumping businesses and motorcycle-equipment manufacturers have huge product-liability risk, while delivery companies have driver accident and misbehavior risk. These risks impact the financial exposure to buyers of these types of businesses.

If you're in a high-risk industry, there's unfortunately not much you can do to change that fact—short of revamping your entire product or service line and pivoting to a new industry—but there are several factors you can make yourself aware of as you consider risk.

The first thing you need to consider is *universal industry trend growth*. A recent McKinsey study looked at the most important factors that impact growth. They found that the first and most important factor is what we call universal industry trend growth. What this means is that if an industry is trending up, then that rising tide raises all ships.[1]

Essentially, those trends serve as tailwinds that push your company higher (as opposed to headwinds that occur when an industry isn't popular).

## Sites That Monitor Industry Trends:

trendwatching.com

trendhunter.com

IBISWorld.com (subscription service)

## Reports from:

*The Economist*

*Forbes*

*Fortune*

If you're thinking of exiting your business, one thing to consider is whether your industry as a whole is trending up. There are several sites that monitor industry trends. My favorites include trendwatching.com, trendhunter.

---

1 Matt Banholzer, Tim Koller, and Laura LaBerge, "How Innovation Can Accelerate Industry Momentum," *McKinsey & Company*, August 13, 2024; and Marc de Jong, Matt Banholzer, Rebecca Doherty, and Laura LaBerge, "How Top Performers Use Innovation to Grow Within and Beyond the Core," *McKinsey Quarterly*, February 12, 2025.

com, and a subscription service called IBISWorld. I also think reports from companies like *The Economist* or *Forbes* can be helpful.

As I write this, the auto industry is expected to have 62 percent growth this year. Auto parts are projected to grow 77 percent. Drugs, biotech, and pharmaceutical are at 140 percent, and education is at 61 percent. On the lower end, food and beverage is only at 15 percent.

Electronics are at 29 percent. None of these industries are doing poorly, but some are trending higher than others.

Obviously, it's good to be in an industry that is trending up. But let's say your industry isn't on an upward trajectory. That's when you have to do some thinking. Sometimes, industries trend down due to natural markets and seasonality. For example, swimwear companies may trend down for a few months during the winter. If you are in an industry like this, then it might be smart to wait a few months or even years to exit. But if your industry is trending downward and you don't see it bouncing back (like if you manufacture palm PalmPilots, for example), then it might be time to get out and let some new leadership step in.

This growth can be measured in what we like to call CAGR, compound annual growth in net income. CAGR is often measured over five years. Similar to exit multiples, CAGR can also be measured using cohorts. For example, if a group of 100 SaaS companies grow an average of 15 percent per year over a five-year period, their cohort CAGR is 15 percent.

## Case Study: How Industry Impacts Exit Multiples

Let's take a quick look at a company I helped with an exit process in the beverage industry. As they were looking to exit, we found a cohort of forty-one companies in the industry. The cohort's CAGR was 15.28 percent, which is nice, positive growth. Using this CAGR, we can estimate that a company in this industry is likely to experience positive growth of approximately 15 percent every year, which means you can anticipate greater than 60 percent growth over the coming five-year period.

Now, this specific company had grown their net income 3.42 percent and revenues 12 percent over the past year. Because that aligned with the CAGR of the companies in the cohort, the expected future growth and revenue of this company meant it was able to command a higher multiple than one that was underperforming industry averages.

## Risk Factor Two: Deal Size

The size of your deal—which is, essentially, the size of your company—is another risk factor that impacts the exit multiple. To be fair, this can feel like a bit of double jeopardy for smaller companies.

Companies with lower earnings and therefore lower profits also garner lower exit multiples.

The reason for this is simply that a smaller company carries more risk. We've all heard stories about companies flatlining or going bankrupt after the first few years. Many, many companies—including some I've worked with and even acquired—have what it takes to launch a product and sell, but haven't established themselves enough to truly scale. This is okay.

I love acquiring companies like this because I know I can turn them around. But they do carry a certain level of risk.

The flip side of this is a large company that, say, has been doing $5 million in sales for the last five years has probably gotten their product, business ops, and marketing all worked out. It's pretty hard to scale to a large profit number without having all of your ducks in a row. The level of risk is lower.

Deal size is one way that you can impact your sales price exponentially. If you spend some time growing your revenue, you can get a higher multiple. There are certain thresholds that give big bumps, so if you are close to a threshold—namely, $1 million, $10 million, and $50 million—it's often a good idea to consider spending a few months (years?) growing. A push or a sprint to cross that threshold can make a huge impact when you exit.

## Risk Factor Three: EBITDA or SDE Size

EBITDA size and deal size are similar in a lot of ways, but I categorize them separately because there are distinctions. Deal size is based on the overall revenue of the company and the overall sales price, whereas EBITDA and SDE size is simply profit.

As you learned in the last chapter, EBITDA and SDE are essentially ways to describe the profits that a company is making. And as you are well aware, a company that makes $10 million in revenue, but spends $11 million to get there, is losing money. So both deal size and EBITDA or SDE are big risk factors when it comes to being Exit-Ready.

EBITDA or SDE size is a risk factor, like deal size, because the smaller the profits, the greater the risk. I'll make it really simple: A business that is making $10,000 is one bad sales cycle or product mistake away from slipping into the red, where you spend more money to keep the business afloat than the business is making.

One product flaw that causes you to issue multiple refunds.

One sales mistake that makes revenues drop.

One market correction.

A similar company with a $1 million EBITDA can more easily weather bumps in the road because they have profit margin to spare. This is why multiples aren't the same for every company, and why smaller EBITDA or SDE numbers garner smaller multiples.

## Case Study: How EBITDA and SDE Impact Multiples

Here is a range of data points for manufacturing companies that shows how deal size impacts multiples.

- Companies with an EBITDA of $0–$999,999 garner a multiple of 3.9.

- Companies with an EBITDA of $1 million–$5 million garner a multiple of 4.5.

- Companies with an EBITDA of $5 million–$9.9 million garner a multiple of 6.3.

- Companies with an EBITDA of $10 million–$24.9 million garner a multiple of 7.

- Companies with an EBITDA of $25 million–$49.9 million garner a multiple of 8.1.

- Companies with an EBITDA over $50 million often hit a multiple of 10.

- Companies with an SDE of $50,000 garner a multiple of 1.25.

- Companies with an SDE of $100,000 garner a multiple of 2.

- Companies with an SDE of $200,000 garner a multiple 2.5 to 3.

- Companies with an SDE of $500,000 garner a multiple of 3 to 4.

- Companies with an SDE over $1 million garner a multiple of 3.25 to 4.25.

While these leaps (especially at the bottom of the chart) may seem small, the dollars add up. Think of it this way: Half of a multiple (.5) is a half year of profit, so if your profit is $5 million, that equals $2.5 million. That's not pocket change. The numbers only go up from there. Imagine doing $10 million a year in sales, and then getting a 3.3 times bump in multiple, which is a $33 million increase.

## Risk Factor Four: Industry Diversification

Because industries can go up and down depending on various (often uncontrollable) factors, one of the ways to decrease your company's level of risk is by diversifying into more industries or even sub-industries.

One way to do this is by looking at segmental growth. Sometimes a segment of a company grows at a dramatically faster pace than the industry the company is in.

### Example: Apple and the App Store

While the smartphone industry has seen steady growth, innovation has slowed in recent years. However, Apple's App Store has experienced explosive growth, far outpacing the broader market. This success can be attributed to several factors.

First, the App Store fostered a thriving ecosystem of app developers, leading to constant innovation and a rapidly expanding library of applications. Secondly, the platform benefited from a powerful network effect: As the number of app users grew, so did the attractiveness of the platform for developers, creating a virtuous cycle.

Finally, Apple generates recurring revenue through app purchases and in-app subscriptions, creating a stable and growing income stream.

This example illustrates how a single segment within a company can achieve significant growth, even in a mature industry, by capitalizing on innovation, leveraging network effects, and identifying sustainable revenue streams. Specifically, it demonstrates how a single segment (the App Store) within Apple's business has significantly outpaced the growth of the broader smartphone industry.

Key takeaways from this example highlight several crucial factors for business success.

First, even within mature industries, companies can achieve significant growth by identifying and capitalizing on niche markets or innovative product lines. Secondly, the growth of a particular segment can often be self-reinforcing, creating a powerful "flywheel effect" where success breeds further success. Finally, the ability to identify and successfully cultivate high-growth segments is a critical skill for companies looking to outperform their industry peers. By recognizing and nurturing these high-growth areas, businesses can unlock new avenues for revenue and drive sustained success.

If you have one segment that is outpacing the others, then it's a good idea to focus more attention on the section that's growing fast. This will help you not only to grow but also to possibly be classified in a different industry, or at least the sub-segment of that industry that is performing better than the industry as a whole.

Another way to do this is through *acquisition*. For example, a recent chart showed a 2.5 multiple was pretty standard in the healthcare and biotech industries with under $999,999 in EBITDA or SDE. On the same chart, the media and entertainment industry had multiples as high as 5 for the same size companies.[2]

That means a company in the media industry will get 2.5 times more money than a similar-sized company in biotech. So how can you turn a biotech company into a media company? One strategy I've used is to acquire a health media company and start using it to boost your biotech business. It helps business, but it can also boost a multiple.

Whatever you do, the *more* diverse you are when it comes to industry, the more likely you will be to weather ups and downs in the market, and as a result, your risk will be lower.

## Risk Factor Five: Ownership and Management

I've mentioned this a few times before but I want to be crystal clear about it here: If your company is owner-operated, the level of risk goes up, and therefore, the multiple goes down.

Why is this?

There is often an assumption that if a company is still owned and operated by the founder, then it is small and lean. People also assume that if a company

---

2 BizBuySell. "Business Valuation Multiples by Industry." Updated with sales from Q3 2020–Q2 2025. Accessed February 2025.

hasn't gone through multiple owners or multiple acquisitions, it must be stable. After all, if one person has managed to keep hold of the company for a long period of time, that person has obviously made profit on it and done well.

This is somewhat true. Oftentimes owner-operated companies are stable and profitable. The pool-cleaning company that has been around for twenty years has been successful supporting its owner for two decades. It has longevity and a history of profitable operations. So does the local laundromat that's been there forever, the gas station, the bakery, the hardware store, the tax-preparation firm, and so on.

The risk of acquiring an owner-operated company comes with the fact that a percentage (often a large percentage) of the transferable value *is* the owner-operator. This person knows the secret sauce and has been able to manage and grow the company. Oftentimes, when a business with an owner-operator is sold, that business faces some pretty big bumps as the new operations team gets up to speed.

Some people want this. They want to take the reins from an owner-operator and use that secret sauce to make their own secret sauce. But a large percentage of investors—especially anyone in private equity—want to buy companies that can operate themselves. They don't want to have to step in and run the company. Instead, they want it to be professionally managed, so when ownership changes, nothing changes about the way the business runs.

Because of this, a company that is owner-operated often garners a much smaller multiple than one that is professionally managed.

## Reducing Your Risk

In my work as an Exit-Ready consultant, one of the first things I do with my clients is help them assess their risk factors and see which ones we can reduce.

Obviously, no one can change their industry, but businesses can pour money and resources into arms of their companies that are in different industries. They can also wait out a seasonal downturn in their industry and sell at a time that is more beneficial. Profits can be grown. Ownership can be transferred. SDE and EBITDA can shift drastically with a few operational tweaks.

All of that said, being Exit-Ready often means some form of waiting and making tweaks before selling. While this waiting and tweaking can be frustrating for owners—especially owners who are emotionally ready to exit—this can make the difference between a multiple of 2 and a multiple of 15.

We've discussed exits, numbers, multiples, and risk factors in the context of several deals that I've done as owner and as advisor or attorney. You've seen everything from events companies to e-commerce businesses, ATM manufacturers to tax firms, and everything in between.

The rest of this book is going to be about how you can make these little tweaks to bring in higher multiples, more money, and better exit terms.

*Part*

# Two

## GETTING
## EXIT-READY

CHAPTER *5*

# GETTING EXIT-READY

Over the last few chapters, I've given you a crash course on exits.

In chapter 1 we discussed the five exits of an entrepreneur (and discovered that you don't necessarily have to exit the company completely to benefit from an exit financially).

In chapter 2 we discussed how to calculate your "number." Ideally, you've figured out how much money you'll need to ensure your company will still sustain you financially, even after the exit.

And in chapter 3 we discussed the complicated (albeit really interesting) process of multiples, SDE, and EBITDA, before covering risk factors and transferable value in chapter 4.

Now that we *understand* exits, it's time to get Exit-Ready.

Companies don't have a price tag. It's not like there's a "business" store online where people scroll through companies, trying to find one that fits their budget. That's laughable. Instead, the same exact company can be acquired for price points that range greatly at multiples from 2 to 15 more.

Because of this, we're going to look for ways that founders can essentially reverse engineer the process so they not only greatly increase the sales price of their company, but also so they can set up the new owners for success as they exit. I call this being Exit-Ready.

On the coming pages, we're going to consider eighteen steps that I've used to help owners become Exit-Ready and to greatly increase the sales price of a company. Be sure to spend some time going through these. If you have completed them all, you'll find that your company is not only Exit-Ready but that your multiple (and therefore transferable value) skyrockets.

## Step #1: Exit the Org Chart

In chapter 1, we talked a lot about the five exits of an entrepreneur. As we discussed, most entrepreneurs—especially accidental entrepreneurs—start out as the "doer" of the business. They are the technician, the manager, the trainer, the sales person, the product creator. They are the operators of the business.

There is a mindset out there—I call it the o-myth—that says founders should be working on their businesses. They should be day-to-day, doing all of the operations that are required to run the company. This is what the vast majority of entrepreneurs do and believe, which is what leaves them burned out and exhausted.

I want you to escape that mindset. You should not be the one sweeping the floors, doing the busy work, or managing the business.

Many entrepreneurs spend their entire career working in their businesses and never move to working above the business. They open the store, make the coffee, serve the customers, order the supplies, train the staff. They are owner-operators.

Instead, the very first thing you need to do to become Exit-Ready is to move *above* the business. You've likely already installed systems, created processes, delegated work, automated tasks, and hired employees. If you haven't, we have the perfect way for you to do just that. It's our Scalable Operating System. You can learn more about that at https://Scalable.co.

Now it's time to hire an operator—for you to step back and let someone take over the operations of the business. This is good for you. You are probably ready to ease away from the daily grind of running your business, and hiring an operator who takes care of everything will save you from burnout.

As we discussed in chapter 1, this is not delegating. Exiting the org chart means handing over operations to someone else who will run the business, and *they* will be in charge of delegating.

Some of you may be feeling a bit overwhelmed by the idea of handing over your operations to someone else. I get that. You've probably poured years into this business and you don't want it to fail. Remember: *This is still your business*. It was your idea, your product, your mastermind. You have systems in place. You have standard operating procedures and sales funnels. I know you do because your business wouldn't survive without them.

When you hire an operator, you're not hiring someone to come in and take over and create the business from scratch. You're hiring someone to come in and run *your* playbooks.

If you want to exit—even in the distant future—you need to start working above the business now. You need to hire operators, as well as complete a few other important tasks we're going to discuss, including: securing investors, getting advisors, entering new verticals, and acquiring intellectual property.

But first you've got to get off the org chart, and that might be a little harder than you first imagine. To help, let's do a little exercise. Grab a piece of paper and sketch out a basic org chart.

CEO at the top.

Below that, add a c-suite with a CFO, COO, CMO, CTO, and CRO.

Below the c-suite, add the typical positions that report to them. An accounting team. An operations team. Customer success. A copywriter. A media buyer.

Now fill in the blanks on that org chart. Obviously, you're the CEO, but how many other roles do you play? How many teams do you manage? How many people do you fill in for? The vast majority of CEOs fill at least four or five additional roles. I call this the You-You Org Chart. The instant the CEO gets off the You-You Org Chart, the transferable value of the business goes up 150 percent. Why is this?

If the CEO shows up on the org chart in any capacity, the buyer knows that the first thing they have to do when they acquire the business is replace that role. When you fill multiple roles—and yes, you probably do—then they have to replace multiple roles.

Replacing the CEO and other employees is just a small part of it. That CEO also has the knowledge, the SOPs, the experience, and the strategies to operate the business. If they are gone, there is no one left to run that playbook.

This is why it's important to exit the org chart and replace yourself as operator. You are still working above the business. You still mentor the new operators, show them the playbooks, and otherwise advise. But you aren't on the org chart at all. This is the place where you have the most value.

As we've discussed, this is why professionally managed businesses sell for a much higher sales multiple.

In chapter 3 we saw that owner-operator multiples run at about 2.5 times SDE across most industries. At the same time, professionally managed businesses sell at approximately 4.5 times. That's 180 percent higher for professionally managed businesses.

Exiting the org chart is the number one step in getting Exit-Ready because it's such an easy win for founders. It will allow you to escape the day-to-day and provide value in the place where you can be most valuable, while at the same time creating an automatic (big) boost in value. There's really no downside. Start replacing yourself today.

## Step #2: Get Structured

For many people (at least those who aren't accountants or lawyers), the idea of restructuring sounds daunting and overwhelming. So let's keep it simple: Restructuring a business is essentially thin-slicing the business to maintain momentum. You take that big, giant loaf of a business and cleave it into little slices. These slices—the technical term is *entities*—help protect what needs to be protected and separate the valuable things so that you don't have to sell everything; or, if you do, you can sell the entities with greater value.

Let's look at several strategies you can take in doing this.

### Start by Structuring based on Value Cache

A collection of individual companies often has a greater value than the company as a whole. Because of this, structuring by *value cache*—organizing the business with each part that adds separate value in a separate entity—can often increase the transferable value of your company as you exit. It also allows you to retain parts of your company while exiting others.

In my time acquiring and selling companies, I've found that it's hard to start from scratch. Very often, there are teams, assets, resources, and intellectual property that the new buyer doesn't care about. By structuring with the value of these assets in mind, you can keep things the buyer won't value but that are valuable to you.

We did this when we sold our big annual event that DigitalMarketer used to own. We separated the ownership of the event from the education company. Then, we were able to sell the event but keep the education company that generated the attendees to the event. Eventually, the buyer decided they were also interested in acquiring DigitalMarketer, but we had other plans for it and chose not to sell.

It happened again when I helped a motorcycle helmet manufacturing company segregate its assets into separate value caches. We put the intellectual property, the brand and logos and such, into a separate company from the manufacturing operation. At the time the business sold, the brand and logos were licensed to the manufacturing company. Thus, the buyer did not want to purchase those items. But later, when the buyer wanted to sell to a larger company, their buyer insisted on owning the brand and logos, and we ended getting the original buyer to acquire the brand and logos for eight figures.

A similar situation arose in another sale, this one with a client who created the logos and branding for a major sporting goods company. My client ultimately received a multimillion-dollar buyout of the logos and branding when a large private equity firm came in to acquire the company he designed the logos for. Because those assets were in a separate company, the sale was quick and easy and did not affect the rest of my client's business.

In another example, one of the businesses I own has a holding company. That holding company has other companies attached to it that serve as profit centers. Each of these companies is a separate entity. Then each of the sub-companies has a variety of profit centers.

The holding company owns other companies like Scalable, EPIC, and Scale & Exit.

There are three main "caches" of value that we spin out. The first is profit centers. All of our entities have separate profit centers like coaching programs, masterminds, books, products, services, offers, and events. This book and the related coaching, mastermind programs, consulting offers, and coursework that go with it are profit centers under one of those entities.

When we structure by value cache, the question we ask is whether a certain "slice" is big enough to belong in its own company. If it is, you spin it out. Anything that is pulling in profit (consistently) is a profit center for an entity.

The second cache is tangible assets. These are the physical things that your business owns—everything from desks to computers to automobiles to construction equipment. Depending on how your business works, you may want to separate these items from your actual business so you don't lose them when you exit. For example, if you drive a company car, there is a high likelihood that the new owners who acquire your business won't want that car. They'll just dump it after the acquisition. By separating that car from the business, you get to keep it, and it saves the new owners the trouble of getting rid of it.

This is often true for technology like laptops and desktop computers, as well as things like hard drives, cameras, and video equipment. Sometimes, even office furniture.

Of course, you shouldn't separate anything that the new owners will need to do business. For example, if you own a 3D printer that is used in the normal course of work, you probably shouldn't separate the 3D printer so they are unable to keep doing business.

The final value cache to consider separating is intangible assets. These are the assets that your company owns that you can't touch—your intellectual property like the brand assets, logos, patents, trademarks, and copyrights. These things have significant value, but the new owner may or may not want them.

This is a judgment call and varies greatly depending on the business. For example, I once acquired a company because I wanted the IP address and their mailing list. I was never going to use their logos, their brand, or their content. So before the sale, the company separated those assets so they could reuse them elsewhere.

On the other hand, let's say you own a small e-commerce shop and the logo and branding are all over the products sold on the website. Separating the intellectual property from the brand destroys the brand and takes away the opportunity for the brand to make money in the future. Again, this is a judgment call you'll need to make.

If you're considering separating the intangible or tangible assets from your company, you may want to consult with potential buyers before doing so to get an understanding of what specifically they are looking for (and not looking for) in the acquisition.

### Then Structure based on Objective

Another strategy I have used when structuring a company is to do so by objective. There are many reasons to restructure, so once you understand your specific objective, it can help you to better understand how to slice that company up.

There are actually dozens if not hundreds of objectives you could have for restructuring. I'm going to share the eight most common.

**1. Preferable Laws:** Some states (or countries) have preferable laws in relation to certain businesses. Sometimes it makes sense to create an entity in a state or country that has laws that favor your business or industry. For example:

Delaware has an easy and flexible incorporation process, and no corporate income tax for companies that operate out of state. The law favors the management of corporations over shareholders generally, so managers like to work for companies incorporated in Delaware. Investors like the extensive body of settled corporate law so they do not have to worry about unexpected legal decisions with respect to corporate law.

Texas has a deregulated energy market, access to skilled labor, and financial incentives for renewable energy businesses, which makes it a great locale for energy and tech companies.

Nevada has minimal business taxes, no corporate income tax, and established gaming regulations.

Singapore has a low corporate tax rate, strategic location in Asia, and government grants for innovation. It's great for finance and technology and a hub for Southeast Asia.

Ireland is a member of the EU, has a skilled English-speaking workforce, and offers R&D tax credits. It's great for tech, movies, and pharmaceuticals.

**2. Geographic Diversity:** Many businesses expand into different territories for a variety of reasons. Oftentimes they create separate entities with each new city, state, or territory so if they want to sell one territory, they don't have to sell all. This approach also diversifies their platform so if a challenge arises in one area (say, supply chain issues), they don't have to face the financial consequences in all areas.

For some of our companies, we have distribution centers located in convenient hub areas to make shipping faster, easier, and less expensive.

**3. Different Capitalization Tables:** A variety of capitalization tables (CAP tables) really helps a business to diversity. For example, one owner could own 75 percent in one entity and 25 percent in another. This gives you options as to who owns what and who gets options in various areas, while also increasing your ability and flexibility to sell.

We use CAP tables often to provide incentive equity to operators in expansion companies without giving them equity in the core companies that are in the process of expanding. That allows them to participate in the upside that they create in the new expansion companies without unnecessarily giving them equity and the benefit of your previous efforts in the core or other successful companies.

## Goose & Eggs Capitalization Structure

A capitalization table shows who owns what and who potentially has a claim to ownership in the form of options or warrants. How your CAP table is structured can impact the value of your company upon exit.

I like to recommend what I call a Goose + Eggs structure. In this structure, you and your partners all pay into a holding company (the "goose") that holds all of the operating companies (the "eggs"). That goose then holds eggs in the form of various entities, such as intellectual property, licenses, smaller companies, and more. This is a capitalization table that shows this structure.

**GOOSE + EGGS STRUCTURE**

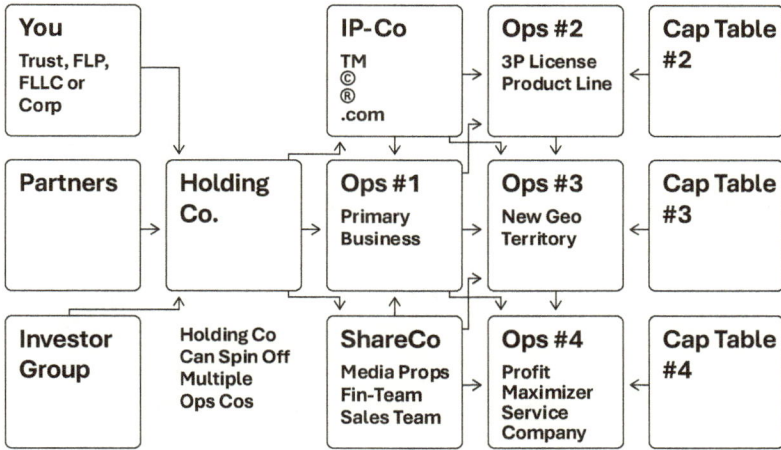

| You | | IP-Co | Ops #2 | Cap Table |
|---|---|---|---|---|
| Trust, FLP, FLLC or Corp | | TM © ® .com | 3P License Product Line | #2 |
| **Partners** | **Holding Co.** | **Ops #1** Primary Business | **Ops #3** New Geo Territory | **Cap Table** #3 |
| **Investor Group** | Holding Co Can Spin Off Multiple Ops Cos | **ShareCo** Media Props Fin-Team Sales Team | **Ops #4** Profit Maximizer Service Company | **Cap Table** #4 |

**4. Maintenance of Control:** The more entities that are packed into your primary operating company, the less control you have. You should always try to maintain control of your most valuable assets. As you start a new thing or move into a new territory, forming new entities allows you to maintain a higher level of control of your biggest assets.

**5. Increase Your Funding Potential:** If you are looking for funding (or ever will), structuring your company in a corporation or at least an LLC makes it much more funding-friendly. Why give investors access to value you created if they are funding a new concept or venture that is spinning out of the company you previously created?

**6. Save on Taxes:** Different jurisdictions have different tax rates. It makes a whole lot of financial sense to hold your company in a favorable tax jurisdiction. Why pay heavy California state taxes when several other states offer no corporate tax at all?

**7. Preparation for Sale:** As you prepare to sell, you need to move anything you want to keep into different entities. We talked about this in strategy #1 (structuring by value cache). Generally, you should consider moving anything you hope to maintain control over, or that the new owners may not want, or that it took you a long time to acquire, into a new entity before selling.

**8. Limit Liability:** By having different entities, you cut off liability at the entity level instead of putting your entire portfolio at risk. Placing higher-risk activities, products, and services in separate entities protects the goose company from liability that may be created in the eggs companies.

Structuring your company—whether by value cache or objective—can be a bit complicated, so I highly recommend you work with a professional business advisor like our team, and your legal team, to make sure everything is in order. That said, taking the time to do this can pay huge dividends; you can make much more money on exit and potentially maintain some valuable assets that you don't want to sell.

## Which Entity Should I Choose?

As I'm sure is clear, structuring a company is complicated. There are not only multiple types of entities—LLCs, corporations, LPs, LLPs in the United States, and more varieties abroad—but also various value caches and various objectives. To help make it plain, the table below shows the most effective structures.

**ENTITY CHOICE: USA**

| Objective Value Cache | Limit Liability | Different Cap Table | Save Taxes | Prefer Laws | Geo Diversity | Funding Friendly | Maintain Control | Prep For Sale |
|---|---|---|---|---|---|---|---|---|
| Profit Center | CORP LLC LP/LLP | CORP | CORP ?LLC? | CORP LLC LP | CORP | CORP | CORP VPS LLC (MM) LP (MP) | CORP LLC |
| Tangible Assets | CORP LLC LP | CORP | CORP LLC LP/LLP | CORP | CORP LP | CORP LLC LP | CORP (PFS) LLC (MM) LP (MP) | CORP LLC LP |
| Intangible Assets | CORP LLC | CORP | CORP LLC LP | CORP | CORP LLC | CORP LLC | CORP (PFS) LLC (MM) LP (MP) | CORP |
| Intellectual Property | CORP LLC | CORP | CORP | CORP | CORP LLC LP | CORP | CORP (PFS) LLC (MM) LP (MP) | CORP |

No legal advise provided: check with your solicitor to determine which type of entity is appropriate for your situation.

## Bonus Strategy: Implement an ESG Program

It seems strange that one of the ways to be Exit-Ready is to implement an ESG program, but I've found that these programs can not only increase the transferable value of a company but also make a company more attractive to buyers.

First of all, what exactly is an ESG program? It stands for:

*Environmental:* Is the company working toward contributing to the world instead of taking away from it? Everything from zero- or low-emissions commitments to ecologically friendly initiatives to any push toward sustainability can contribute to your company's environmental health.

*Social:* Is the company working to make the world a better place for all people? A focus on social justice and on ensuring that all people are better as a result of having worked for or with the company falls into this social bucket.

*Governance:* Is the company managed by an independent board of directors that is responsible for its strategic vision of the company?

This means the ability to govern the business is in the hands of people who have been elected.

After reading the above, you're probably wondering what in the world this has to do with being Exit-Ready. A lot, actually.

First, having an ESG program gives your company a wider appeal. There is a whole universe of buyers, and many of them are looking for companies that are not only profitable but also focused on important issues like equity and the environment. This may become a permanent positive or it may just be a passing trend, but it is good to consider.

Additionally, multiple funds that have raised money to make the world a better place through business will contribute large grants to potential buyers who are acquiring companies that share those values. Having an ESG program in place can assist potential buyers in acquiring funding and purchasing at a higher price.

Finally, a properly structured company with an ESG program can save between 10 to 100 percent in taxes. That's not a typo. Some companies that structured themselves in a way that allows them to focus on their products, as well as the environment and social issues, have been able to save millions in taxes.

These changes can make an impact that could increase your exit value by 2 to 200 percent. (Again: not a typo.)

### *Bonus Strategy: Start a DEI Program or Hone the One You Have*

It is likely obvious to you that this is a good thing. Diversity helps any business to thrive. The science backs it up. Just a few stats to get you thinking:

- Companies with diverse executive teams are 33 percent more likely to outperform their peers on profitability.[1]

- Companies in the top quartile for gender diversity on executive teams are 21 percent more likely to outperform on profitability.[2]

- Companies with more than 30 percent women on their executive teams are significantly more likely to outperform those with fewer or no female executives.[2]

- Ethnically diverse companies are 36 percent more likely to outperform their peers.[2]

- Diverse teams are 70 percent more likely to capture new markets.[3]

- Inclusive companies are 1.7 times more likely to be innovation leaders in their market.[4]

- Companies with inclusive cultures are twice as likely to meet or exceed financial targets.[5]

- Organizations with inclusive cultures are three times more likely to be high-performing.[5]

- Inclusive teams improve team performance by up to 30 percent in high-diversity environments.[6]

1 Sundiatu Dixon-Fyle, Kevin Dolan, Vivian Hunt, and Sara Prince, *Diversity Wins: How Inclusion Matters* (McKinsey & Company, 2020).

2 Vivian Hunt, Sara Prince, Sundiatu Dixon-Fyle, and Lareina Yee, *Delivering through Diversity* (McKinsey & Company, 2018).

3 Sylvia Ann Hewlett, Melinda Marshall, and Laura Sherbin, "How Diversity Can Drive Innovation," *Harvard Business Review*, December 2013.

4 Josh Bersin, "Why Diversity and Inclusion Will Be a Top Priority for 2016," *Josh Bersin* (blog), December 7, 2015, https://joshbersin.com/2015/12/why-diversity-and-inclusion-will-be-a-top-priority-for-2016/.

5 Juliet Bourke and Bernadette Dillon, "The Diversity and Inclusion Revolution: Eight Powerful Truths," *Deloitte Review* 22 (2018).

6 Deloitte Australia and Victorian Equal Opportunity & Human Rights Commission, *Waiter, Is That*

- Companies with higher-than-average diversity had 19 percent higher innovation revenues.[7]

Similarly to ESG programs, DEI programs not only increase your company's ability to make money and scale, but many buyers look to acquire companies that have focused on diversity.

In an era when social justice topics fill the nightly news cycle, and diversity initiatives are making changes across every sector of the market, many potential buyers are looking for companies that place a high value on DEI. Before you get ready to exit your company, it's best to make sure your DEI program is growing and that your team is diverse and strong.

## Step #3: Stop Being the Product or the Brand

If the product is you, or if your brand is you, then you have a challenge.

Think about Tony Robbins. I love the guy. He was a client of my law firm when I practiced law, and I represented him for years. Then after I stopped practicing, I had several opportunities to speak at his Business Mastery events in the US and Europe.

He has a great company and a compelling brand, but it's a hard company to exit because it was built on his name and face. When he did want to exit, he ended up selling his brand to his employees via an ESOP, which may or may not have been a good investment for the employees, but was very likely considerably less favorable to Tony than it would have been if he could have

---

*Inclusion in My Soup? A New Recipe to Improve Business Performance* (2012).

7 Rocío Lorenzo, Nicole Voigt, Miki Tsusaka, and Matt Krentz, "How Diverse Leadership Teams Boost Innovation," *Boston Consulting Group*, January 23, 2018.

sold the business without a dependence on his name, personality, and his personal brand.

The thing is, Tony is a unicorn. He *is* his brand, and it's hard to see how his company will hold transferable value if he exits the org chart or the brand altogether.

Now consider Kim Kardashian. She's a rock star businesswoman who created companies that have made her a billionaire. But how valuable will those companies be if she's not there focusing attention on them? She's a genius right now, but the value is in her personality, her persona. Hopefully, she will leverage the personality brand into independently valuable brands.

When you're the brand, it's hard to transfer the value to another owner without transferring you with it. With the exception of a few industries such as fashion houses, it's hard to carry on without the original founder. If you are or have been the face of your business for a long time, it's time that stops. You have to build real business value outside of you.

For some of you, this step will be easy. You probably already did it in step 1 when you exited the org chart, or even when you first founded the company. For others—I'm looking at you, consultants and mastermind leaders—this step can be very difficult. That said, it's not impossible.

Let's say you run a mastermind and coaching program. You are the face of that business. Chances are, you have several coaching frameworks that you use to help your clients. These *frameworks* have produced proven results and have given your customers reason to invest in your products.

Now the question is: Are you the product, or is the framework the product? The answer can be both, but if you're trying to exit, the first thing you need to do is separate yourself from the product.

This doesn't (necessarily) mean a name change—the McDonald brothers haven't flipped burgers in a McDonald's in the decades since Ray Croc acquired the company—but it means separating what you're selling from you as a person.

I've had to do this in several of my businesses. For example, I have a podcast called *Business Lunch,* on which I invite high-profile guests to talk about— you guessed it—business. We get into the nitty-gritty details about how to run, grow, scale, and exit businesses.

A few years ago, I realized that the podcast was becoming quite lucrative. Several other businesses started approaching me for advertising—which was great—but even better, I found that when I talked about my own products like EPIC or consulting on the show in an organic way, those businesses spiked. That podcast had become a profit center that was driving profits in several other businesses.

So what did I do?

I stopped being the brand.

Did I cancel the podcast?

No way! It's still going and growing. But I prevented my name and face from becoming the brand of Business Lunch. I started this transition by bringing in a co-host, my business partner Ryan Deiss. I also started diversifying the guests, the audience, and the structure so that if, should I ever want to exit, I could do so seamlessly.

I'm still part of the brand, but I am no longer the brand. As we discussed in the introduction, you should always be in the process of exiting.

## Step #4: Differentiate Your Company (Then Create Defensible IP)

What is special about your business? Why should a customer choose you over your competitor? What's in it for them if they work with you?

You don't want to be a copycat of anyone else. (That's just a race to the bottom as far as price. Ask any airline!) Instead, you want to find ways your company is different from others and then demonstrate your differences through defensible IP (intellectual property). But before you rush to create new IP, you'll need to grow beyond your core.

In August of 2022, renowned consulting firm McKinsey conducted a study called *The 10 Rules of Growth* to find out the things that really make a difference in a company's success. One of their big findings was that companies who are always trying to grow beyond their core are more likely to be successful.[8]

Start the differentiation process by having your key stakeholders (perhaps your executive team or your managerial team) get together to brainstorm what distinguishes you from the rest of the market. I use what I call a *competitive advantage worksheet,* but you can also just write it on a white board.

Start by brainstorming your competitive strengths. These are the things you know your company is really good at. For example, maybe you're faster at innovating the newest items, you have a low-dollar test model, you create useful or entertaining content, or you have a known influencer who promotes your brand. Write these items down in a list.

Next, write down what your customer needs and wants. Maybe it's great

---

8 Chris Bradley, Rebecca Doherty, Nicholas Northcote, and Tido Röder, *"The Ten Rules of Growth,"* McKinsey & Company, August 12, 2022, https://www.mckinsey.com/capabilities/strategy-and-corporate-finance/our-insights/the-ten-rules-of-growth.

content, ease of purchase, known brands, low price, or free shipping. Finally, write down your competitors' strengths. Maybe they are cheaper than you, their storefront is in a better location, or they are a huge company with lots of funding.

Once you have those lists, make a Venn diagram. The places where your competitive strengths and your customer wants and needs intersect make your competitive advantage. The place where your competitor's strengths and your customer wants and needs intersect are your vulnerabilities. These are opportunities to grow beyond your core. Finally, the place where your strengths and your competitor's intersect are your table stakes, the place where you have to focus to ensure that you can improve.

This exercise will reveal your strengths and your competitive advantages clearly. What differentiates you from the competition will become plain, as will opportunities to grow beyond your core.

Once you know your competitive advantage, how do you capitalize on it? After all, knowing it and knowing what differentiates

you from the others will accomplish nothing if you keep the information to yourself.

Start with *defensible* IP—intellectual property that belongs to you and that no one else can use. Defensible IP is anything for which you have original rights of authorship. The many types of defensible IP that differentiate one business from another include:

1. Copyrights for books, music, SaaS code, video, courses, ads, audio sounds, or anything else you or your business have created.

2. Patents for useful new devices and processes.

3. Trade secrets. For example, the recipe for Coca-Cola and the formula for which eleven herbs and spices are used in Kentucky Fried Chicken.

4. Publicity. In the US, you have the right to your name, image, likeness, and voice.

5. Registered trademarks (where you see the ® symbol) or pending trademarks (marked with the ™).

6. Any branding such as names, logos, slogans, or even packaging. For example, the blue color on the Tiffany box is defensible IP.

There is a final step in this process: All your defensible IP and awesome differentiation does nothing sitting in your office. You need to get the word out. That's why the final step is to proclaim your wins!

Earned media in the form of PR is a great way to show the world what you have to offer. This will boost your revenue, but it's also a way to distinguish yourself when you begin to exit.

You could seek out recognition for your work by media or companies like the Inc. 5000, Ernst and Young's Entrepreneur awards, or a JD Powers award. Awards like this catch the attention of buyers. If you're on an Inc. list (even for your state or city), you will be inundated with calls from people wanting to buy your business, join your business, and invest in your business.

## Step #5: Replicate and Automate

Let's say you design custom suits and create a bespoke suit for every person who comes into your office. This is hard to scale. You will have one busy tailor and if you start to grow, you will have to bring in new tailors, each with their own ideas and styles. You need to replicate and automate so you can deliver a high-quality, standardized result.

The best way to illustrate this idea is to compare the two shoe brands Nike and Reebok.

Nike started with a runner—Phil Knight—and his coach. Phil loved to run and started experimenting with shoes to find out which shoes helped him run the fastest and stay the most comfortable when he ran. Once he figured that out, he decided to expand. He went to other runners—first high school and college runners and their coaches, then professional runners and their coaches. From there, he found influencers in the sport who helped him by endorsing the shoes.

Once Nike was dominating the running shoe market, they decided to move on to basketball. But they didn't start from scratch. Instead, they replicated the process they had used for developing their running shoes. They started with basketball players and coaches. They tested designs and worked out the kinks. They made it so people started talking about them. Then they found some professional basketball players—ever heard of Michael Jordan?—to endorse their products.

From there, Nike systematically went from sport to sport and ran their playbook for developing shoes. They replicated their processes for tennis, football, baseball, soccer, and so on.[9]

Reebok, on the other hand, became famous in the 1980s during the aerobics boom.[10] They had great shoes, and the aerobics crowd seemed to love them.

---

9 NIKE, Inc., "Recasts Segment Financials in Connection With the Consumer Direct Offense," September 25, 2017 (press release).
10 Olivia B. Waxman, "How Jane Fonda Helped Inspire Reebok's Freestyle Fitness Sneaker," *Time*, April 30, 2018.

What they did not have was a replicable system.

Instead, they went to market opportunistically. If they saw an opportunity, they jumped on it. They expanded haphazardly into several different sports but with no solid, replicable plan. They tried all sorts of marketing, but there was no unifying, repeatable plan. Nothing was done systematically.

Now, as I write this book, Reebok is a footnote on the bottom of the financial statements of a private equity firm, relegated to near obscurity, while Nike is one of the most valuable companies in the world.[11]

The lesson? *Replicating your playbook will help you to create value so much faster than opportunistic market decisions.*

What's more, a buyer will place a premium on the processes that you have developed versus a company that's always wondering what they are going to do next.

Once you have created replicable processes, it's time to automate. Automation will allow you to standardize a particular result.

Automation is the process of asking: How can we reduce our dependencies on labor, while trying to get our expenses down?

There are four main ways to do this:

7.  **Implement software processes.** Code never sleeps. It never takes a day off or asks for a raise or calls in sick. It's automated. It can scale infinitely. Of course, you have to keep it up to date and manage it, but one of the best ways to automate is to install software processes that can replace labor and reduce dependencies.

---

11 Authentic Brands Group, "ABG Finalizes the Acquisition of Reebok," Mar. 1, 2022 (press release).

8. **Amplify human performance with AI.** One of the best examples of using AI to amplify human performance is in the copywriting space. If you don't know, copywriters write emails and marketing messages for ads. A good copywriter is very hard to find and very expensive. They often take a percentage of the income they generate. Recent advancements in AI have created copy proven to be more successful and perform better than the copy written by most humans. With copywriting AI, you essentially get the brilliance and brains of amazing copywriters and have effectively automated it. You will need a human to manage the process, but AI can amplify that human's work to a higher level than it would be otherwise. This helps you spend less, and get more done. We use this in all of our businesses to make our copywriters more efficient and effective. We create ad campaigns using Google Gemini, Open AI Chat GPT, and Anthropic's Claude. Using HeyGen, our copywriters can automatically generate videos creative with AI-generated versions of us. Our AI avatars can answer text, audio-, and video-based questions using Delphi. The opportunities are virtually limitless.

9. **Employ robotics and machines.** Obviously, robotics and machines do a lot of work in factories and on assembly lines, but if you dig deeper, you'll find that robotics programs can also automate some of the rote, repetitive tasks your staff is doing. This makes your staff happier— they can get more "real" work accomplished—and it makes you more efficient in knowing your future staff needs. We hired an RPA (robotic process automation) firm to completely automate data entry for our tax return preparation company. It does the data capture and entry tasks in minutes that used to take days for our human employees to complete.

10. **"Productize" your services**. If you provide customized services,

then your business is hard to automate. Early on, my co-founder Ryan Deiss offered a "Let Us Build Your Marketing Funnel for You" service through our company DigitalMarketer. It got a lot of attention. Developing a marketing funnel is hard, and everyone wants the pros to do it for them. The problem was, it wasn't scalable. Our crackerjack marketing team spent all their time building funnels for other people. Without hiring tons more marketers, we just weren't making enough money. We built a significant business, but it didn't scale. So we decided to "productize" it. Through a product called Million Dollar Napkin, we created a product version of the ideal funnel. Rather than building funnels for people, we showed them how. We took our IP and turned it into a product that has since scaled into multiple other products and profit centers.

It probably feels a bit strange to be talking about ways to scale right now when you're reading about exiting. You may be wishing you had this information years ago, or that you had been able to use these tools early on. But here's the thing: I'm not asking you to invest years and years into creating a scalable company. You could. And it would make your company more profitable. But even taking small steps toward removing yourself as the brand, creating defensible IP, and then replicating, automating, and productizing will pay big dividends when you exit. You don't have to do these things perfectly, but even a little can make a big difference. (We have books, coaching, and courses on Scalable.co.)

## Step #6: Shift or Pre-Capture Cogs

Many business owners have to find a constant balance between scaling and capital. This is a huge challenge—owners have to pay the cost of goods, labor, or marketing before they can get money from their customers.

If they want to scale quickly, they have to invest additional capital. They have to hire more people, buy more products, increase their ad spend. On the flip side, if they pull back on spending, they also slow down scaling. It often takes quite a bit of capital, and that can require the business to take on debt.

When you're getting Exit-Ready, you often want to grow fast—to increase your profits and revenue so you can get a higher multiple and a higher sales price.

When I'm working as a consultant with a client who wants to be Exit-Ready, I ask if it's possible to shift the burden of the cost of goods sold (COGS) so that they still scale. Essentially, so they can *pre-capture* those costs. This means they are able to finance the costs of goods prior to selling them without taking on debt or losing equity.

One of the best ways to do this is by adding some sort of recurring revenue.

As we discussed in chapter 4, recurring revenue will garner a multiple that is much higher than a standard one. (Remember, ARR is the holy grail!) Recurring revenue will also allow you to pre-capture COGS. This is a key component of leveraged sales—it creates automatic sales each month without much effort.

I'm sure you've noticed that subscription boxes have taken off in the last few years. This is why. Why go back to the same customer each month (or quarter) to sell them a new product when you can pre-capture that sale? And why resell them on each new course you create, or on each consulting package you offer, when you can sell them a recurring package where they pay on a monthly basis for access?

There are other ways to shift and pre-capture COGS.

We used to have an event called the Traffic & Conversion Summit (until we sold it). This was the huge event I mentioned earlier in the book that cost us millions of dollars each year, between booking the space, paying for speakers, and other costs. It would be a huge financial burden on the company to lay out all these millions of dollars and then wait to recoup it until the actual event.

The solution was simple: We asked all of our vendors if we could make deposits on the costs. Then we started offering super early bird and early bird tickets, giving us money to start paying those deposits.

By continuing to sell tickets early (with discounts) and selling sponsorships to exhibitors who wanted access to our audience, we were able to generate a large percentage of the money from early ticket sales and sponsor costs.

Another example of this is Dell Computers. They sell their computers before the computers are built—you order the computer and it is then built to your specifications. If you buy it in the store, it may cost more, or have less features. Dell pre-captures your money before they spend money on parts or labor.[12]

The ultimate pre-capture is Kickstarter. Often people pay years before the product they are supporting is delivered. Kickstarter campaigns capture in advance the money needed long before the product is ready.

Think about this in your business, and you may find you don't need as much capital and loans and debt as you thought. Ultimately, pre-capturing COGS will allow you to scale much more quickly than you might have anticipated.

---

12 Joan Magretta, "The Power of Virtual Integration: An Interview with Dell Computer's Michael Dell," *Harvard Business Review*, March–April 1998.

# Step #7: Design, Curate, and Measure Customer Experience

What does the customer experience when they interact with your business? While customer experience (CX) has always been a big part of doing good business, it has recently become a key performance area that is really important to buyers.

If you're not currently measuring your CX, and using the data to improve it, then you're missing out on an opportunity to get a premium upon exit. In fact, one recent statistic I read on *Forbes.com* said companies with better CX have approximately 5.7 times higher valuation.[13] But you can't just say "I want to have a higher CX" and make it happen. CX has to be designed and curated. Let's look at a few ways to do just that.

### *Customer Touchpoint Inventory*

I recommend taking what we call a Customer Touchpoint Inventory. Basically, on a piece of paper (or spreadsheet), write down all the places that your potential customers come into contact with your brand.

Ads

Walk-by

Print

Email

Search Engine

Webinars

---

13 Blake Morgan, "100 of the Most Customer-Centric Companies," *Forbes*, June 30, 2019, https://www.forbes.com/sites/blakemorgan/2019/06/30/100-of-the-most-customer-centric-companies/.

Landing Pages

Retargeting

Social Media

Then go through each touchpoint and discuss how you're curating that experience. When a prospective customer sees an ad, do they click through to a landing page that is clear, concise, and drives them to the product or content you want them to see? When they add something to a cart and purchase, do they get a good follow-up email? Do they have to log in to buy or is there a guest checkout? Are there one-click upsells? Are the webinars informative and directing them to the right place?

A few weeks ago, my wife became aware of an upcoming sale at one of her favorite stores. Before the sale, she spent a week researching the products she liked, carefully selecting sizes and colors, and deciding what she would buy. The day of the sale, she got up to press "purchase" only to find out that the company didn't have a persistent cart. They had a three-day stick period, so her entire cart was emptied. She gave up in frustration, and what would have been an easy, large sale for the company ended in a lost sale.

Every company should be thinking about touchpoints like this. You must be conscious of the ways customers are interacting and consider how to curate the experience. You are the steward of your brand, and your customers should feel like every interaction they have with you is exactly what they needed.

Perhaps the most overlooked aspect of CX is a customer's post-purchase experience. Most companies have a nice thank-you email and send a receipt, but I challenge you to consider how else you could touch the customer post-purchase. Perhaps it's a messenger confirmation. Maybe it's tracking and text alerts for delivery. Maybe it's an unboxing video or an email with uses of the product. Perhaps it's a loyalty program or a reorder campaign. Whatever it is, post-purchase touchpoints are a great way to improve CX.

### Fab 50 Outreach

Another method we use to design and curate CX is what we call a Fab 50 Outreach. For this, you choose fifty customers—they can be random customers or your fifty best customers, but fifty people who have recently purchased from you. Then, you send them a short survey asking questions about their purchase.

We call this a Fab 50 because the questions we ask them are about their feelings, actions, and beliefs about the company.

How did the product make them feel? Did it reduce stress? Has it made their lives easier?

What actions did they take with the product? How did they use it? How will they use it in the future? Will they purchase again? Refer a friend?

What beliefs do they have about the product? Did it influence their life in a positive way?

The answers to these questions can help you curate your CX in a way that will inform the feelings, actions, and beliefs of future customers.

### Measuring CX

Customer experience needs to be measurable for it to affect your exit multiple or price. The most common way to measure CX is through a *net promoter score*, or NPS. An NPS is a measurable way to show buyers how happy your clients are with your business, and how likely they will be to maintain those clients should they purchase.

To determine a net promoter score, customers are asked one simple question: On a scale of 1–10 (1 being the lowest), how likely are you to refer a friend to the business? People who respond with a 9 or 10 are considered promoters. They will promote your business to others. People who respond with a 3–8 are disregarded. And people who respond with a 1 or 2 are considered detractors.

From there, subtract the average detractor score from the average promoter score to get a net promoter score. I'm not going to tell you how to do the math exactly because there is affordable software that can do it at scale.

It's worth noting that in addition to NPS, many companies are measuring eNPS—employee net promoter score. Instead of asking the question of how likely someone is to refer a friend to the business, the eNPS asks how likely an employee is to refer a friend to work at the business. This score can also improve exit value and multiples as the buyer knows that the company is a place where many people would want to work.

By doing your due diligence in both curating and measuring CX, you'll be able to increase your NPS. Companies will pay a premium for that. You will get your deal done and make more money from your exit.

## Step #8: Create M(A)RR

I realized the value of M(A)RR when we were discussing the acquisition of one of our companies a few years ago. The buyer looked at all of our revenue streams and offered us a multiple of 1 on the standard revenue, but they offered 4 times for our revenue that was recurring. A lightbulb went off: In terms of getting more income each month, when you have recurring revenue, the money just comes in. You don't have to go out and get those sales.

### *Legitimate Recurring Revenue*

There are several kinds of legit recurring revenue, some better than others. I'm going to list them from the least appealing (but still good) to the best.

11. **Consumables that must be replaced.** Think of printer ink. If you run out, you have to replace it. On these consumables, there is no contract or auto-billing (typically), but simply the fact that you have a product that is used up and must be replaced. There are various options for replacing it, but customers will often return to the original source for more.

12. **Sunk-money consumables**. Sunk-money consumables are items that have some component that must be replaced, and that component must be replaced by you. Razor blades are a good example. Buying an actual razor is cheap, but the blades are more expensive and each type of blade has to fit a specific razor. So once someone has bought your razor, they will come back to buy more blades as needed.

13. **Manually renewable subscriptions. These** are subscriptions that must be renewed on a regular basis. Magazine subscriptions or mastermind memberships are great examples.

14. **Sunk-money subscriptions.** A sunk-money subscription is one where a renewal must be made through the business. An example is a Bloomberg terminal, a box with special connections that delivers data.

Once you have the box, you must renew the data-delivery subscription on a regular basis to continue getting the data.

15. **Auto-renew subscriptions.** An auto-renew subscription is like a cable bill, phone bill, or HBO. The customer pays for the service on a monthly basis automatically and they have to call and cancel with notice to stop paying it.

16. **Contracted term subscriptions.** These subscriptions are auto-renewed but they aren't month to month. For example, with an email service provider, you contract with them for a period of time (like two years) to pay a monthly fee.

17. **Contracted term with auto-renewal.** Even better is a subscription that has an automatic renewal after a contracted term.

### *How to create M(A)RR*

Here's a helpful exercise for creating M(A)RR. Write down the top income streams that you have in your company. Maybe they are software, physical products, courses, events, coaching, and masterminds. From there, write down whether the income stream is static or recurring.

Then, go through each of the static revenue streams and consider how to make them recurring. The most common ways are things like a buyer's club, SaaS, memberships, or renewals. From the list above:

**Software:** SaaS products are often recurring. You could offer a training program with monthly training courses on use, a certification on using that software that has a renewal.

**Physical products:** Physical products make great subscription box products. This is also an opportunity to create a buyer's club where they get new products automatically every time they update. This works great for products like wines that have frequent new releases.

**Courses:** Create a monthly membership that grants access to the courses, or an automatically renewing certification on people who complete the course.

**Coaching:** Create a retainer on coaching that allows your clients to receive an automatically recurring ten hours a month.

**Masterminds:** Create a program that allows customers to attend all mastermind events for a discounted rate.

Spend a few hours figuring out all the ways you can create recurring revenue from what you already have. We've been able to successfully do this with several companies I own. One example is our War Room product. War Room is a mastermind group where we really dig in with some of our most successful founders about how to scale and grow businesses. We started it as an add-on day to certain events, but we found that it became increasingly popular with every event. So we made it a recurring product. Now people pay an annual fee and get to come to every War Room event, as well as receiving additional virtual sessions and other benefits.

Remember, you don't have to make your entire business M(A)RR. There are some things that people just buy once and that's it. The idea isn't to throw out the static profits, but instead to see which products can be converted to M(A)RR so you can be Exit-Ready and have a higher transferable value.

## Step #9: Get Leveraged Sales

As we discussed in chapter 1, most businesses have sales and profits. (They wouldn't be in business for very long if they didn't.) But I believe sales and profits aren't enough.

Companies should focus on garnering *leveraged sales* and *earning bankable profits*. If you don't have them, then you have no transferable value and you aren't ready to exit. Here are some ideas for turning that situation around.

**Twenty Quick Wins to Get More Leveraged Sales**

1. **Create bundles and multiples packages.** Bundle a few of your top-selling products together, or add a discount when people purchase multiples. This increases the average order value and creates incentives for people to buy more items.

2. **Extend your value ladder.** Look at all the things that someone can purchase from you on their customer journey. Now see how you can expand it. Is there an expensive product you can add to the top of your value ladder? Or a firewall product that will keep them from going to other places? Or a low-ticket item that will get them in the door so you can start ascending them up the ladder?

3. **Optimize your traffic channels.** Look at all of your traffic channels—at my last count there are forty-two of them—and tick off the boxes where you are advertising or marketing your product. Are there opportunities to expand into new channels or optimize the ones that are doing well?

4. **Expand into adjacent markets**. At one of my companies, we sold

a tool called a credit card knife to preppers. We realized that outdoor enthusiasts, fishermen, and hunters would also like that knife, so we expanded to additional markets. You can also expand to an adjacent geographical market—for example, you could start in the US and then add selling in Canada, or start in L.A. and then go to New York and fill in between.

5. **Price test and use applied pricing.** If you aren't constantly testing your prices, you don't know if you're getting everything you can from your sales. Use applied pricing, or the ability to change your price for the same thing as it's packed in different ways or sold in different channels.

6. **Convert expenses into profits.** Spend some time looking at your cost centers such as your content team or paid media team and figure out how to turn those into profit centers. For example, you could sell content services or paid media services to a third party to cover expenses for your in-house team.

7. **Find ways to get zero-dollar traffic**. Find someone who has already aggregated your target customers into a list or group and acquire that list or group to get a whole new source of traffic.

8. **Expand through rapid methods of expansion**. Some traditional methods like franchising or licensing can be effective in creating leveraged sales.

9. **Expand through strategic ventures or partnerships**. Joint ventures to co-promote products or events, or long-term strategic relationships, can be quick wins for leveraged sales.

10. **Try a product integration.** American Airlines partnered with Casper

to provide mattress pads, duvets, pillows, blankets, and other sleep amenities in Flagship First and Business class. A whole lot of wealthy customers got what is essentially a "free trial" of Casper products.[14]

11. **Add or expand an affiliate program.** Affiliate programs create incentives for people to sell your product for you, meaning you do less work and make more sales.

12. **License other people's products.** Start selling other related products (or even bundling your products with other products) or allow other companies to license yours.

13. **Bolt-on business.** A few years ago, we did a bolt-on with Infusionsoft, a CRM email and marketing cart business. We bolted on our content marketing ability to their business and fed them the leads they wanted. It ended up being a $50,000 annual revenue stream for both companies.

14. **Vertically integrate your supply and distribution chain.** Look at who you are paying for outsourced products or services. See if you can acquire the people who are getting some of your profit margin, or integrate those tasks into your existing business.

15. **Borrow a sales force.** One of my companies sold motorcycle helmets. I knew of a motorcycle manufacturing company that had a full team of reps working all markets, selling directly into stores. We worked out a deal that for a percentage, their reps would sell our helmets into the same stores.

16. **Create recurring revenue.** Bundle items or services, and create a recurring revenue model. See steps 6 and 8 in this chapter.

---

14 American Airlines, "American Airlines and Casper Help Travelers Dream Big With New Suite of Onboard Bedding," Sept. 29, 2017 (press release).

17. **Add digital products to your physical products.** An author I know wrote a book about the college application process. She sells her book for $14.99, or if someone pays $25.99, they get the digital book plus a "digital bundle" immediately mailed to them with essay questions, prompts, and other materials.

18. **Add physical products to digital products.** A yoga teacher I know has a training platform with digital yoga classes. When people purchase recurring access to her class, she sends them a yoga mat and some weights to use during her class.

19. **Add services to digital products.** You could sell a tech support subscription with a SaaS product or paid marketing training to a paid marketing contract.

20. **Micro M&A for growth.** Acquire or merge with smaller companies to expand your reach or list.

Each of the above ideas is a quick way to expand your leveraged sales. If you tackle several of them, your leveraged sales, and therefore bankable profits and transferable value, will increase rapidly.


## Step #10: Increase Bankable Profits

Oftentimes companies take their profits and roll them right back into the company. This isn't a bad thing. It's good to invest in scaling your company. But ultimately, your company is there to serve you. Which means that beyond your salary, you should have bankable owner distributions to save, invest, or use for the things you want to do.

To get bankable profits, you need to increase your current profits. I have created an entire training on this. If you're interested, head to Scalable.co and search "SPV Framework." In this book, I will give you some quick steps to optimize your profits.

There are six categories (or areas) in which profits can be optimized. In my course, I suggest that people make a simple chart that includes an action to be done to optimize profits in that area, along with a current cost, a target cost, target savings, and an implementation date. If you choose one or two from each area, you will improve your bankable profits significantly.

### Area 1: Time-Based Profit Improvements

In this step you adjust timing to push costs away, or accelerate the receipt of revenues. The bigger the gap between when money comes in and when you have to pay for costs, the less money you have to work with.

*Examples:*

Resist the temptation to pay invoices the moment they come in, and instead wait until their due date.

Send out invoices for receivables immediately.

Take deposits on large orders or orders that will take a long time to fulfill.

### Area 2: Labor-Based Profit Improvements

In this area we focus on efficiencies and how fast your team can get things done. Are there ways to increase speed without impacting effectiveness? Your objective is to work to maximize your labor force in a way that also maximizes flexibility.

*Examples:*

Work with managers to find efficiencies that you can create with your labor force. Ensure that people aren't doing the same tasks.

Identify sources of wasted time. For example, do employees wait for heavy machinery to start up or for materials to arrive at their work area?

### Area 3: General Profit Improvements

These are just what they sound like: general improvements—ways you can boost profits by increasing margins or cutting costs.

*Examples:*

Increase your markup on certain products by just a few percentage points.

Experiment with selling price to maximize profitability.

### Area 4: Supply and COGS Profit Improvements

Cost of goods sold can vary greatly based on your supply chain, so in this area you look to adjust costs of goods to enhance profitability.

*Examples:*

Find a more affordable supplier for one of your main product components and increase profit margins.

## Area 5: CapEx-Based Profit Improvements

Capital expenditure improvements, or CapEx-based improvements, consider the things you must buy—the hard assets you must spend money on—to operate your company. This is everything from the office you sit in to the manufacturing lines or divisions you need to create your products.

*Examples:*

Move to cheaper office space to save on rent.

Move to a geographical location that has lower labor rates.

Find a manufacturer who can decrease manufacturing costs.

## Area 6: Cash-Based Profit Improvements

In this area, focus on improving your cash flow to optimize your profits. Consider how you can manage your cash flow more wisely to increase the amount of cash you have at any given time.

*Examples:*

Extend accounts payable to net thirty days and then forty-five days to defer costs.

Move your cash into higher-interest accounts to earn more.

Get deposits for large orders.

# Step #11: Simplify Offerings

## Roland's Book Recommendations

*Simplify* by Richard Koch and Greg Lockwood

This book is worth reading if you want to simplify your business to maximize profit. The authors worked with a research firm to compile data on what successful businesses do, and based on those findings they give specific ideas on how to maximize business success.

Have you ever had feature creep on one of your products?

Maybe you're in a meeting and someone says, "You know what, it would be cool to add this..." And then the next week a client says, "Well, we would buy it if only the product had that..." So you add more features, more bells, more whistles, and soon you have a product with some really great stuff—but a whole lot of unnecessary features.

Any amount of complexity adds costs to a product. On the flip side, if you are able to eliminate costs that your average customer doesn't care about, then you can increase your bankable profits or lower the sales price or both.

One of the first people who became known for thinking this way was the great entrepreneur Alfred Sloan. He worked for General Motors and put together what he called "a car for every purse and purpose" —a brand/price ladder that matched models to customer segments, with step-ups in features and price. These cars aimed to minimize overlap, with each tier designed for a specific customer.[15]

---

15 The Henry Ford. "Advertisement for General Motors, 'A Car for Every Purse and Purpose.'" Collections & Research. Accessed October 24, 2025.

For example, the base Ford Model T was very simple and affordable, while GM offered a progression from Chevrolet upward through Pontiac/Oldsmobile and Buick to top-tier Cadillac (Oakland existed earlier and was later replaced by Pontiac). Cadillac's were loaded with features, and cost a fortune.[16]

Sloan's architecture allowed GM to target each customer based on what they needed and wanted. Features that weren't wanted by certain customers were taken out, and different vehicles were designed for different customers to satisfy different types of demand.

A modern master of this architecture was Steve Jobs and Apple. There was a time when Apple was lost and floundering. They didn't have market share. People didn't love their products. They didn't have a handle on what their customers wanted. At that point, their product range was all over the place. They had seventeen (!) kinds of Macs, each with different features and components.

Steve Jobs decided to simplify. He asked: Who is our market? The answer was twofold: professionals who needed computers to help them do their work, and home users who wanted computers for simple tasks like word processing and games. So Jobs cut 70 percent of Apple's products. The Apple product suite became four computers:

- iMac Desktop
- Power Mac
- iBook
- Powerbook

Apple simplified to two desktop computers—one for consumers and one for

---

16 Encyclopaedia Britannica. "General Motors (GM) | History, Deals, & Facts." Accessed October 24, 2025.

pros; and two laptop computers—one for consumers and one for pros. Those four products changed Apple's entire trajectory and helped it become one of the world's most valuable companies.[17]

They later applied the same strategy to the iPhone.[18] Cell phones had keyboards and slide screens and power banks and gaming screens and all sorts of things. iPhone took all the features away and gave customers exactly what they wanted:

- **A Touch Screen.** At that point, most phones either had a T9 typing system or a fold-out keyboard. With Apple's touch screen, anything conceived of in software could be displayed on the screen with no need for additional hardware.

- **More Battery Time and Memory.** Apple phones don't have a million buttons or ports to plug in various things. Yes, this created turmoil with the people who didn't want to buy iPhone connectors, but it reduced the weight of the phone, allowing more space for memory and battery. It was a worthwhile tradeoff for 99 percent of the population.

- **Bigger screens.** Free of keyboards and buttons, iPhone screens got bigger and bigger. I used to carry my iPad everywhere so I could access spreadsheets and watch video, but with the advent of bigger full-screen iPhones, the need has disappeared.

- **Bluetooth Headphones.** All the audiophiles in the world who love their fancy headphones hated it when Apple got rid of the headphone jack, but now AirPods have become a standard part of most people's technology collection, and the phones are even lighter and more

---

17 Walter Isaacson, *Steve Jobs* (New York: Simon & Schuster, 2011).
18 Brent Schlender and Rick Tetzeli, *Becoming Steve Jobs* (New York: Crown Business, 2015).

flexible.

- **Cameras.** iPhone cameras have lots of lenses and great quality, eliminating the need for anyone to carry a camera.

Apple's iPhone is simple…and exactly what phone users want.

For most businesses, 20 percent of the products and services are responsible for 80 percent of the sales and profits. It's time to double down on those top 20 percent and get rid of or improve the 80 percent.

To simplify, start by looking at your products that aren't performing as well as they could be. Got a product that you can't deliver at scale? Scrap it. A service that sucks all your time and energy? Toss it. If a component of your business has gotten over complicated and clunky, simplify it. Do an analysis to see what can scale, and what needs to go.

### What Products Should Be Eliminated or Changed

There are seven main reasons that products tend to underperform, and therefore should be either jettisoned or simplified. Products that:

21. **Cannot Be Delivered at Scale:** Some items are just hard to scale. Consulting is an example of this—you as an expert consultant only have a given number of hours in a day. If you're consulting forty hours a week, you can't exactly scale that to four hundred hours a week.

22. **Are Incapable of Being Productized for Uniform Delivery:** If a product is expensive or hard to produce, or if it's custom, then it's hard to create and deliver to your clients in a uniform way that is profitable.

23. **Are Unable to Compete:** If someone else owns the market and the

price points, then you probably can't compete. This can also happen if someone has an entrenched position, if they have intellectual property that you need to make your product, or if they have a 90 percent or higher share of the market. You can't compete, so get out.

24. **Have Low Profitability:** I work with a client who had two main customer segments: small businesses and consumers. There is a huge market for his product in the small business space, but its profitability in the consumer space kept declining. Wisely, the client decided to emphasize the more profitable small business arm so their focus isn't diluted.

25. **Have Low Value for Customers:** This may seem harsh, but if your product has low utility or low fulfillment value for your customers, it's hard to get a good price or make a profit.

26. **Are Obsolete**: If a product isn't useful anymore—think tracking software for a video rental store—then you probably shouldn't keep it in your product line.

27. **Have a Declining Market Share:** If you're losing market share over and over, and you can't find additional markets where the tide is rising, then your profitability is sure to decline as well.

By cutting unnecessary features from products, or dropping underperforming products from your product line, you can ensure that you increase your bankable profits.

## Step #12: Scale and Cross-Train Teams

One thing that's often overlooked when founders are looking to exit for maximum value is the team that's left behind. One of the primary concerns for someone looking to acquire a business is the level of risk. They want to know if their acquisition will be worth their time, effort, and money.

And one of the biggest risks in any acquisition is whether critical labor—the people making things happen in that business—are going to become unavailable. Buyers want to know that they will be able to continue doing the things that the business does even after the founder is gone. By scaling and cross-training your teams, you ensure any buyer that if a given person becomes available, the business will continue to run.

Honestly, this is something that you should probably do as a founder whether you are exiting or not—replacing key employees is hard, and having people cross-trained ensures that you will have time to refill key roles without losing productivity. If Tiffany in accounting does all of your order processing, you don't want all orders to stop being processed if Tiffany decides to retire or finds another job. You want someone else on your team to be able to step in and do the job until Tiffany can be replaced.

To cross-train my teams, I use what I call the Employee Cross-Training Tool—essentially a chart that has every job title on my teams in column A. Then I have my managers list out which employees hold those titles, their tasks that should be cross-trained, who should be cross-trained, and a training date.

The important thing is that you are thoughtful and efficient on who and when to train. For example, Tiffany's order-processing task probably shouldn't be done by a content marketer or a videographer; the skill set is very different. But perhaps a sales support specialist who processes all sales would have similar skills.

For the purpose of this example, let's say that your sales support specialist is named Calvin. You identify Calvin as the one to be trained on order processing, set aside time for Tiffany to teach Calvin how to do all of your company's order processing, and have Calvin cross-train Tiffany on all sales processing. That way, Calvin and Tiffany both know how to do that component of each other's job. If either leaves or is gone for any amount of time, both sales and order processing will still happen.

But there's a catch: You don't want to train Calvin to do all of Tiffany's job. That would mean that if Tiffany leaves, Calvin would be doing two jobs. And to be honest, Calvin isn't Tiffany. He has a different job and a different skill set, so while he can do some of her work, he's probably not the exact fit to do all of it. Instead, I recommend that you cross-train based on job tasks.

Let's say Tiffany is also responsible for accounts payable. AP is very different from order processing or sales processing, so it makes no sense to train Calvin to do it. But Julia, the accounts receivable clerk, does several tasks which are similar. So have Tiffany cross-train Julia on accounts payable, Calvin on order processing, and so on.

Something else to consider is technology. For example, most accounting software comes with a certain number of seats. You probably have a seat for everyone in your accounting department, but not for anyone in your marketing department. If you're cross-training an employee on an accounting task, it's a good idea to train someone who already has a seat so you don't have to spend money to buy another seat.

One other warning: Don't plan on doing all your cross-training on the same day or days. I did this once and while my entire team got cross-trained, we lost three days in a row of production time. It's probably best to set aside small chunks of time—maybe an hour for Tiffany to train Calvin on order processing one day, then an hour for Calvin to train Tiffany on sales processing the next.

Once you're done with all the cross-training, create a matrix with all of your job titles and tasks and then write down who has been trained so that if someone is gone—even if it's for a vacation—you know who else can complete each task. The last thing you want is for Calvin to go on vacation, and then have none of the sales get processed that week.

By having a cross-trained team, you essentially eliminate the risk of a business slowdown or (worse) shutdown should someone leave. The truth is, when a founder is exiting, there is a risk of others leaving as well—turnover often invites more turnover—so the more capable your team is of taking tasks and keeping the machine running, the less risky the company is to acquire.

## Step #13: Add Experienced Managers

This one may be common sense, but I've found that oftentimes the things that are the most logical are the ones we most often forget: You need to make sure you have experienced managers.

One of the biggest fears most buyers have is that their new acquisition will fail as it moves forward. They don't want to take a risk on a company that could go under or decrease in profitability. They are worried that when the founder leaves, the company won't grow at the same rate. The buyer wants to know that you have the team in place capable of hitting the numbers in the months and years to come.

By installing experienced managers—managers who have longevity in the industry and with the company—the risk is lowered. You know that when the founder exits, someone who knows what they are doing can take the reins in any given department.

The best possible scenario for management is that each department head has seen the next two levels of growth. I call this the rule of 1's and 3's. For example, if your current sales are $10 million, it would be great if you had a management team in place that had seen growth to $30 million, and at least one manager who had seen growth to $100 million.

The most important experienced manager is a Chief Operations Officer who has a strong enough background and experience to step in as CEO when you exit. After that, if you have someone who has seen the next two levels of growth leading your marketing team, your sales team, and your finance team, then you are sitting on one valuable company.

Of course, that may not be possible, but at the very least, you should have someone with as much experience as possible in each of those areas. This begs the question: If you don't have those people on staff, how do you get them?

It's certainly not easy to hire an experienced, capable leader, and finding multiple at the same time can be complicated. If you already have someone on your team who has seen those levels of growth but maybe isn't in a leadership position, it might be time to promote them or train them.

If you don't have someone on your team, start searching. Get your human resources team to post the job and find some great candidates. If you have to, pay them 20 percent more than industry standard in your area to make sure they have the incentive they need to come over. This will pay off in terms of what you can get to exit, so hire them. It will be worth it when you are able to sell for a much higher price.

## Step #14: Add a Long-Term Retention Plan

In the previous step, I advised you to make sure you had experienced managers in place so that any buyer will feel confident there is a solid team that can ensure the company will continue to grow and hit its numbers. This step builds on that. As you surely know, no team can function with managers alone. You need well-trained, experienced, ambitious, smart teams in place to get the work done. How can you make sure that you are able to keep key employees?

Current cultural trends have people job-hopping every couple of years. Add an acquisition or merger and the exit of a CEO to the mix, and there's a risk that large parts of your team could leave if you exit. People leaving—especially key people—is risky. It's not only expensive to replace them, but with a new acquisition, it leaves the buyer exposed to a loss in productivity that they might never recover from. New people may not know how to perform the tasks at hand, and new managers won't know how to train them. Additionally, it costs a lot of money to find, hire, and train talent. By adding a long-term retention plan, you incentivize your team to stay in place even as you exit, and you can ensure that the buyer will have key people as they take the reins.

As you consider a retention plan, here are some questions to answer:

- How are you compensating key people in the company right now?

- Can you afford to pay 10–20 percent above current market rate for key people?

- What other incentives do you offer to key employees?

- What are your current benefits packages and how do they stand out from similar companies?

- Are there any other ways you can be competitive in the HR

marketplace?

Once you've thought about your answers, consider how you can use that information to ensure that your key employees—anyone who would be hard to replace—stay. For example:

- If your pay scales are at or below market, can you afford to give everyone a raise?

- Can you afford to pay your key managers or leaders above market value?

- Could you offer supplemental benefits like health insurance, wellness benefits, fertility benefits, or companion care benefits?

- Is your revenue sharing or bonus structure competitive?

- Could you expand your 401(k) or retirement benefits?

**Roland's Book Recommendations**

*Motivation-Based Interviewing: A Revolutionary Approach to Hiring the Best* by Carol Quinn

This book shows people who hire teams how to differentiate the best candidates so that they can land high-performers who will stick with the company. By using motivation-based interviewing techniques, you can hire and integrate people into your company in a way that creates loyal, long-lasting teams.

**Eight Easy Ways to Improve Employee Retention**

1. **Increase your eNPS Score.** You should always be monitoring your employee satisfaction—because if you don't know how your employees are feeling, you won't know how to retain them. One tool

we use is the eNPS: the employee net promoter score (as discussed in step 7 of chapter 5). The eNPS asks employees how likely they would be to refer a friend to work at that company. A good score means your employees are happy enough to want their friends to join them. A lower score means you need to work on your company culture. By monitoring employee satisfaction, you are able to see how engaged your employees are in the business, and how likely they are to stay.

2. **Get Your Employees Involved.** Sometimes the best long-term retention plans cost nothing. Simple things like having regular stand-up meetings to share information, acknowledging good performers, and having good internal communication can greatly improve your company culture and employee retention. Make sure your employees always know where the business is going, who is doing well, and what good you are doing for your customers and for the world.

3. **Create a Formal Employee Recognition Program.** Giving employees an opportunity to earn incentives can vastly improve retention. These incentives don't have to be big-ticket items like a trip to Hawaii. They could be a simple shout-out at a meeting, an employee-of-the-month parking spot, or a small gift card.

4. **Provide Opportunities for Professional Development.** Give your employees the chance to attend workshops or conferences or training to gain key skills. This will not only help them to do their job better but also show them you are willing to invest in them.

5. **Make Upward Career Paths Clear.** Everyone wants to move up in their career, so make it clear to all employees what their path is to promotion, and what they need to do to get there. This could include providing opportunities for people to learn about upward career paths

through management training or cross-training so staff can see the trajectory that they are on.

6. **Get Serious About Culture.** We talked about this earlier, but one of the best ways to keep key employees is to make sure your company is a place where people want to work. Create opportunities to bond as teams through off-sites and events. Offer fun workplace perks like Friday lunches or a weekly on-site espresso truck. Think about ways to build camaraderie.

7. **Offer Compelling Benefits Packages.** We also mentioned this before, but one of the best ways to get competitive in the employment market is to be competitive—by offering higher salaries and compelling benefits. Figure out what you can do to provide the best health plans and supplemental benefits for your employees.

8. **Offer Merit Bonuses or Equity.** Give your employees an opportunity to earn equity in the company through merit so they have an incentive to stay and an incentive for the company to perform well.

By doing the above things, you can ensure that key employees are willing to stay and help your buyer to keep your company growing.

## Step #15: Document Systems, SOPs, and KPIs

You have an amazing team that does an amazing job at what they do. I know this without knowing anything about you because any business that has scaled and grown to the point where the founder is able to exit has to have an amazing team. But your amazing team that does amazing things is only as strong as the systems and processes you have in place.

For example, let's say you have an amazing receptionist named Norah. Norah answers phones, transfers calls, knows how to handle customer complaints, hands out mail, and manages the company-wide schedule. Norah is amazing. But let's say Norah decides to retire and move to Colombia and live on the beach. Lucky Norah!

Depending on how you have documented systems, standard operating procedures (SOPs), and key performance indicators (KPIs), Norah's departure could be a minor inconvenience...or a major catastrophe for your business. Likewise, if you haven't documented the systems and SOPs so anyone can come into the business and replicate them, you're setting your buyers up for a big struggle.

**What is the Difference Between a System and an SOP?**

A *system* is the way you do things as a business. For example, you may have a standardized system for accounting that uses QuickBooks for all accounting practices like accounts payable, accounts receivable, and inventory.

The SOP, or *standard operating procedure,* is how you accomplish the tasks in your systems. For example, your accounting SOPs would include how to open up QuickBooks, naming conventions, which days you do accounts payable, and who each invoice is sent to.

With this in mind, in this step we are going to document our systems (how we do things) and our SOPs (the step-by-step operating procedures for each task) and then take those systems and SOPs and document how we measure progress toward goals through KPIs. In other words, you need to document how Norah answers the phone, how Norah transfers calls, how Norah handles complaints, etc., so that when someone comes in to replace her, the brand experience is consistent and the new person will know exactly what to do.

Documenting systems and SOPs can be daunting if you haven't done it before. It's not as simple as writing down everything you do every day—and it's certainly not making a giant binder of step-by-step rules that no one will ever read. Usually the end result is somewhere in between. If you just get started by writing down one process, you can create your SOPs bit by bit, action by action. For example, have Norah write down the ideal process for receiving an inbound call, e.g., how many times should it ring before being answered, then what to you say when you answer the phone. That's the first SOP for inbound call handling. Then, have each employee, in this case Norah, build on it from there one process at a time as they do their day-to-day job.

My first recommendation is to give it time. If you try to rush this documentation you will find yourself at a complete standstill, and you will probably miss important steps. Plan on spending twelve months documenting all jobs with SOPs, and then task your managers with the job of working with their teams to roll out SOPs in a strategic way.

At one of my companies, Scalable.co, we spent several months developing a detailed process for documenting systems and SOPs. I'm not going to explain the entire process here, as that would take several chapters, but if you would like to know more, head to Scalable.co and search for our Scalable OS offerings.

The key is to avoid getting so lost in the process of documenting that it damages your company. Instead, it should be a thoughtful, patient, team effort. Take time to review the SOPs and hone them into the right systems and SOPs. This way you have good checks and balances and your systems and SOPs can evolve with your company.

## Documenting KPIs

As you're documenting your systems and SOPs, it's easy to get into the weeds about how to do things like answer phones or file paperwork, but if those systems and SOPs aren't leading toward performance, then they are just a bunch of tasks.

The second part of this step is to find ways to document your KPIs through a KPI dashboard so your team and any future buyer will know exactly how progress toward goals is made. A KPI dashboard provides future owners or leaders with insight into what everyone is doing, and how those tasks are measured against the company's goals.

At Scalable, we have done a lot of work on this, and if you want in-depth access to our processes and tools, look up the Scalable OS on Scalable.co. That said, I will do a high-level overview here.

We start by doing quarterly strategic planning. During that planning, we first determine our goals in key areas like sales, profit, NPS, eNPS, and then we determine the leading and lagging indicators of success. For example, let's say your goal is to increase sales by 10 percent each quarter. If your sales are currently $3 million per quarter, then you need to earn $3.3 million to hit 10 percent. But $3.3 million is a huge number, and just throwing it out there is not only daunting but also leaves your team wondering how to get there.

By creating a dashboard that measures progress incrementally, you're able to show your team the step-by-step process to increase sales 10 percent per quarter. In this example, sales are currently $3 million, and 10 percent of 3 million is $300,000, so our targeted sales number is $3.3 million. If you divide $3.3 million by three months you need to sell about $1.1 million each month to reach your goal. If you want to go even further, you need to sell about

$275,000 each week to reach your goal. What gets measured, gets managed. By creating a dashboard so your team can measure progress each month (or more frequently), you're able to monitor progress and ensure that if you start to fall behind, you are able to make changes to catch up.

It's also a good idea to look at lagging and leading indicators. For example, weekly sales are a leading indicator for quarterly sales. You know that if you're getting $275,000 per week, you are likely to hit your goal of $3.3 million each quarter. Sales is a lagging indicator of the number of sales conversations that your team is having. The number of conversations is a lagging indicator of the number of leads being brought in. You can get really granular and say that you need X number of leads each week in order to schedule Y number of conversations in order to hit your weekly sales targets.

By working backwards, you are able to measure exactly what your team needs to do to hit the company's goals.

## Strategic Growth

The point of having all of these systems, SOPs, and KPIs isn't to make sure things run the same way even after you're gone—and in most cases, it's probably a good thing if they don't.

No, the point of having robust systems, procedures, and goals is to ensure that a buyer knows your company has strategic growth. Yes, you have grown and scaled, but the buyer needs to know that the growing and scaling was intentional and purposeful, and that it is repeatable.

If you have your systems, SOPs, and KPIs clearly documented and measured, you are able to take steps to ensure strategic growth. There are lots of ways to be strategic with growth, a few examples being:

- **Strategically allocate resources based on what is performing best.** Let's say your marketing team is spending ad dollars to generate leads for three different products. They are splitting the ad spend up into thirds so each product gets 33 percent of the money. But let's say you notice a trend that one of those products is getting four times the sales and four times the profitability. Then you can reduce the ad spend on the other two products to 10 percent, increase the spend on that one product to 80 percent, and for the same number of dollars, you'll start making incremental progress toward your goals.

- **Invest in capital expenditures to improve performance and value.** Capital expenditures—or the equipment, land, office, cars, and other materials that help your company do what it does—can be strategically used to help you scale. For example, let's say you have an old machine that produces your product, and while it is effective, there is another machine that could produce your product in less time with fewer mistakes. By investing in that new machine, you stay at the forefront of customer satisfaction and give your buyer something of value that will improve productivity for a long time.

- **Use your debt and cash flow to scale.** If you are able to predict sales coming in and cash flow, you can use that knowledge to improve your company. Perhaps you have a low debt ratio and lots of incoming sales, you can invest in other acquisitions or capital assets or team members. If you need to increase your debt to fund your business, then you will be able to predict the best ways to use debt and cash to grow your business.

I'm sure you get the idea, but when you're thinking of exiting your company, and you want to exit at the highest value, the better you can measure what is going on, and manage your systems, SOPS, and KPIs, the better equipped your team will be to continue scaling and hitting numbers even after you exit.

## Step #16: Diversify Your Customer Base

Let's say you own a company that sells T-shirts. You started by selling a T-shirt here and a T-shirt there, but then one day T-shirt megalith T-Shirts-R-Us comes to you and tells you that they want to sell your T-Shirts in all of their stores. You're suddenly cranking up production, sending thousands upon thousands of T-shirts to stores around the country, and raking in the profits. Your margins go through the roof and everything is amazing, right?

Well, sort of.

Yes, of course, it's great to get a big customer who places big orders. But when it comes to exiting, if every single sale or a large portion of your sales are coming from one source, it can make a buyer uncomfortable. It's a risk for a buyer to purchase a company that doesn't have a diverse customer base. Lots of things change when there is an acquisition—and sometimes customers decide to make changes when the owner does. If losing that one customer would make a huge impact on the business, then the buyer stands to lose a lot of money.

The 10 percent rule says that you really don't want any single customer to be responsible for more than one-tenth of your total revenue or profit. You want a diversified revenue stream with many customers, none of whom are responsible for more than 10 percent of the money you bring in.

For example, if you have 1,000 customers and 999 of them have an average order value of $10 per month, but one single customer pays $100,000 per month, then that one customer can make or break your entire business. They are less than 1 percent of your customer base, but more than 90 percent of your profits. This is likely to raise a red flag.

To make a buyer comfortable, you also need to have diverse sources of customer acquisition. If every single customer you get comes from Facebook ads, but then Facebook changes its algorithm and your leads plummet; or if every single customer you get is from your personal networking, but when you leave the customer pool dries up; then the buyer is taking big risks by purchasing your business. In order to make a buyer comfortable, you need to find ways to diversify your customer base. Let's look at two ways to help you do just that.

### Create Predictable Selling Systems

As I've mentioned, at Scalable we have a Scalable OS system that involves creating predictable selling systems. This is especially important when it comes to an exit, because the buyer wants to be able to predict with relative confidence that products and services will continue to sell.

One example of an *un*predictable selling system is word-of-mouth. You never know who is talking about what and when they are talking. What's more, you can't predict when word-of-mouth conversations will happen. On the other hand, word-of-mouth can become a predictable selling system if it is formalized. Imagine a system for generating referrals after a practice. Perhaps you ask people to refer three people when they do a review. Maybe you even give rewards or thank-you gifts for referrals. That is predictable—you have a system in place that you know will generate results.

There are lots of predictable selling systems. A paid media campaign will result in a predictable number of leads based on the dollars you spend. When you advertise on a podcast, a given number of listeners will respond at a predictable (albeit estimated) rate.

The more predictable your selling systems are, the more leads you have coming in that you can predict will convert. And the more different selling systems you have, the more diverse your customer base is.

## Traffic Gap Audit

To start, you need to know how you acquire customers—who is coming in, and from where—so you are able to predict who will continue to come in and from where. I would start with what we call a *traffic gap audit*. Begin by looking at your highest ROI traffic channels for generating leads and/or customers, such as:

- Email
- SEO
- Paid Search
- Instagram
- Facebook
- YouTube
- TikTok
- Offline Direct Response
- Affiliate

Go through your list and write down how much traffic came from each of those sources in the last quarter. If a business gets one hundred thousand leads from

Instagram but none from TikTok, it often leads them to assume that they should go all-in on Instagram and drop TikTok. This makes sense in a way: You should definitely not invest large amounts of time and money into channels that aren't working for you. But before you toss TikTok, do some testing. Evaluate the content you've been sharing, along with other social media metrics. If you started posting videos on a weekly basis, would more people convert? Are there other ways to optimize TikTok? Because if you can get TikTok to work, that's a whole new stream of new customers.

If you look at your traffic gap audit and see that a large percentage of your traffic comes from one or two sources, then you know it's time to expand into other areas. By expanding, you diversify your customer base and ensure that a buyer will see that no matter what happens—an algorithm changes, an affiliate drops, an email campaign fails—they will still have a predictable stream of customers.

## Step #17: Review and Audit Financials

Every buyer is going to want to review your financials before they acquire your business. One of the best ways to eliminate risk—and therefore increase your sales price—is to have good, clean financial reporting.

I know what you're thinking: *Of course* we have that! Every business has that. It's true. If your business has been around for any period of time and has been even marginally successful, you should have financials ready and available—a balance sheet, a list of liabilities, and details on owners and equity. These are good—don't get me wrong—but these are simply a snapshot of a given moment in time. They tell the buyer the assets you had, the balances you owed, and the negative equity in the business as of the date you sent the financials. This is great information and you should absolutely send it, but if this is all you have to send to a potential buyer, you are going to end up getting a much lower multiple for purchase. Why? Because the buyer is only getting a glimpse of your financials, which puts them at much higher risk.

For this step, you need to do a complete audit of your financials, so the buyer can get a full, accurate picture of what they are acquiring.

A note of caution: The picture you get from a full financial audit could make your financial numbers look worse. For example, your balance sheet could be higher and your liabilities lower at a snapshot point than they are after a full audit. Even so, a full audit will likely help you garner a higher sales price because your multiple will increase when the financials are clear.

Even without a higher multiple, you want to operate in good faith and make sure that any buyer is getting exactly what they are paying for.

So how should you do this audit?

Whoever conducts it should go through all of your balance sheets, invoices, receipts, payments, and so on, over the last few years and put together a full financial portrait of your company. In addition to the balance sheet, list of liabilities, and details on owners and equity, you'll want to have them include the following:

1. **A Profit and Loss Statement (P&L):** This is a measurement of all of the income you have received minus all the expenses leading to a profit or loss over a period of time. This can generally be done on a monthly or quarterly basis, but your financial reviewer should put together P&Ls for at least the past twelve quarters if possible.

2. **A Statement of Cash Flows:** There are lots of things in accounting

that aren't actual cash expenses. Things like depreciation, revenue recognition, amortization, taxes, and interest (remember our discussion about EBITDA?) are all expenses that impact the revenue and profits of a company, but don't relate to operations. Because of this, the definition of profit on income statements is different from cash in the bank. A statement of cash flows shows how much actual cash is coming in at a given time.

3.  **YTD Financial Statements:** You need all financial statements for the year to date in question.

4.  **Three-Year Financial Statements:** If possible, try to get financial statements for the last three years.

Even if you have an amazing bookkeeping department, you will probably need to spend some time getting your financials reviewed and audited before you exit. To do so, here are three options, each one better than the next, in order of good, better, best.

## Option 1: Full Internal Review and Audit

You can do a review and audit of your financial statements internally. This is good—it will give the buyer a good picture of where the business stands and will allow you to dive into the financial operations of your company. If you have an internal bookkeeper or accountant or CPA, they can essentially open the shoebox of receipts—figuratively, but maybe literally as well—and check all of your finances. They can compile all of your financial information, conduct any research to validate it, and then put it into a statement that gives a buyer a full picture of your finances.

## Option 2: External Accountant Review

I recommend engaging an outside accountant to review and audit your financials. It's better than an internal review for one simple reason: It means someone else helped you. Someone else looked everything over and, with an outside perspective, was able to catch any mistakes or oversights.

I want to note here that this is in no way meant to undermine your team or its internal review. In the same way that even the best writers don't edit their own writing, the best accountants shouldn't audit their own finances. An outside accountant does due diligence to see if the numbers are valid. They aren't warranting the financials. They aren't guaranteeing that they are perfect or correct, but they review them to ensure that they are accurate to the best of the accountant's knowledge.

## Option 3: Professional Audit

A professional audit of your financials lowers the buyer's risk the most and thus will give you the highest possible exit price. Audited financials allow the buyer to trust the financial statements, as an outside source has not only reviewed the financials but also verified and warranted them. Because of this due diligence, the buyer can be sure that the statements they have are accurate.

This is obviously a much more expensive option, but for the people taking the risk to acquire the company, it puts them at ease. It means that an outside expert has thoroughly looked over all of the books *and* done their due diligence to double-check the numbers.

Another thing to think about when considering an audit: Buyers will put more faith in a regional or national accounting firm. Yes, you can get your good old Uncle LeRoy who happens to be a CPA to do your audit. Uncle LeRoy is great, but if you engage a large, credible regional or national firm, a buyer will feel much more comfortable. While I recognize that a full audit by a national firm isn't possible for some business owners, I recommend that you do the highest level of review you can within your budget.

**Pro Tip: The Easy Accounting Tip That Can Earn You Millions!**

Once you have reviewed or audited your books, look for a Forward Twelve Months multiple (FTM) instead of a Trailing Twelve Months multiple (TTM). There is usually a range of multiples that buyers will pay for businesses in an industry, and an FTM multiple is possible. If you have clean financials that go back twelve months, and you can prove that your past projections have come to fruition, then you can at times get a multiple based on the FTM instead of the TTM.

For example, let's say you own a digital marketing agency. Agencies in this industry tend to trade for a 5 or 6 times multiple of EBITDA, which means the buyer is going to pay 5 to 6 times what your profit was in the last twelve months. If your EBITDA was $1 million last year, you can likely fetch $5 million to $6 million for the business.

Let's say you've projected 20 percent growth each year for the last three years and have realized that 20 percent growth. Let's also say you're projecting 20 percent growth yet again. If you are able to get a multiple on the FTM—$1 million + an expected $200,000 from 20 percent growth—then your multiple is 5 to 6 times that. That would make your exit price $6 million to $7.2 million. By having good financials and proven projections, this agency could make $1 million more on the sale, which is equal to a full year of profits.

## Step #18: Use Micro M&A For Growth

Helping businesses make acquisitions is kind of my thing. Mergers & acquisitions (M&A) are what get me excited and what keep me up at night scheming new plans and ideas. I have an entire business—EPIC Network—that sprung out of the idea that acquisitions can lead to business growth and expansion. I'm especially interested in Micro M&A: small businesses acquiring other small businesses to grow their current businesses, boost their portfolios, and become Exit-Ready.

I'm not going to get too in-depth on this step in this book because I've already written, developed related coursework, and created a mastermind group on this exact topic. If you're interested, head to epicnetwork.com to learn more.

That said, while I'm not going super deep, I would be remiss to not discuss micro M&A somewhat because I believe it is perhaps the most important, most impactful, and quickest way to grow your profits so that you can exit. Through strategic M&A, you can literally double your traffic, quadruple your list, quintuple your output…overnight. In fact, you may be imagining that as you exit, whoever is buying your company will take the reins and mom-and-pop it to the next level, but I would venture that a good percentage of potential buyers are looking at your company as their own opportunity to grow and expand. As you look to exit, you will garner a higher multiple if you have proven that you get it, and that you have been able to successfully acquire new companies to grow your own.

I think of it twofold. First, by acquiring companies, you demonstrate that you understand the game. You know how mergers and acquisitions work. Second, while you're demonstrating that knowledge, you are also growing your business a whole lot faster than you would organically.

Micro M&A is the act of acquiring small companies or lists or platforms to merge them with your larger company and help both companies succeed. This generally means that you acquire properties valued at less than $100,000, although there are times you can go higher than that. But in this step, I'm not suggesting that you try to acquire Apple or Meta. Instead you go after the owner of that Facebook group that has 10,000 followers in your target market, or that SaaS company that makes the exact software you need to increase your production.

### Pro Tip: Increase Your Multiple and EBITDA...Overnight

One cool strategy that I've seen used very successfully is Enterprise Value (EV) Acquisition Arbitrage. EV means you look for businesses in industries that garner a lower multiple, you acquire them, and then you merge them with your higher-multiple business. This makes all of the EBITDA earned from the lower-multiple business eligible for the high multiple.

For example, let's say you own a professionally managed business in an industry that trades at or near a 6 times multiple, such as a business formation company or a real estate brokerage. You know of an owner-operated business that is in a similar industry, but one that trades at a 2 times multiple, like a small law firm or almost any other owner-operated company. If that business has about $1 million in profits and you acquire it at 2 times—so, $2 million—and then merge it with your business, when you exit, that same exact business and profit line can get a 6 times multiple. You literally made $4 million overnight.

Enterprise Value Acquisition Arbitrage is an easy and often overlooked way to increase the value of your business significantly.

## The Acquisition Wheel

There are several types of acquisitions. Acquiring a storefront is different from acquiring a media property, which is different from acquiring a SaaS product, and so on. I like to break the types of acquisitions down by the reasons people acquire. I call this the Acquisition Wheel. On the wheel, I sort acquisitions by the goal you are trying to achieve. My recommendation is to go through the wheel and determine if any of these can help you reach your goals, and then figure out how to most effectively use these acquisitions to grow your company.

### Acquisition Wheel Category One: When You Want More Customers

Every business needs customers. As a general rule, the more customers you have, the more sales you make, the more profits you earn. So naturally, one of the main reasons businesses do M&A is to get more customers. There are lots of places to get customers—paid media, organic traffic, outside sales, advertising—but far and away the fastest way to acquire new customers is to acquire competitive businesses. By doing so, you essentially obtain all of that business's customers (and their product) and increase your revenue in the process.

### Case Study: How A Small Window Shade Company Acquired the Competition

There are several types of competitors.

### 1. Direct Competitors Who Sell to the Same Market

By acquiring a direct competitor with a similar-sized business who sells to the same market, you can essentially double profits and sales overnight.

For example, if you own a window shade business and you sell window shades to homeowners who are seeking to block sun and ensure privacy, you could acquire that other window shade business across town and literally get every single one of their customers at once. You'd also get access to their advertising channels, traffic sources, perhaps a storefront, and their product.

## 2. Indirect Competitors Who Sell to A Similar Market

Let's say there's a business in town that sells window shades only to small businesses and offices. If you acquire that business, you are able to expand your customer base to include businesses in addition to your current customer base of homeowners.

## 3. Indirect Competitors With a Geographically Different Platform

Maybe there is a window shade company that does great business in the next state over. Maybe you acquire them so you can expand into a different town or market. The same is true for the digital or online space. Maybe you own a storefront, but you want to expand into the online market, so you acquire a window shade company with a huge digital store.

## 4. Indirect Competitors Who Offer a Service You Want to Offer

There is a company in town that specializes in installing window shades that people have purchased elsewhere. By buying this company, you can streamline your window shade operation and offer a new level of services while obtaining that company's customers who may, in turn, buy your window shades.

## 5. Indirect Competitors Who Offer a Substitute For Your Product

There are lots of levels of products. If you offer standard, middle-of-the-road privacy shades, but there's a company that sells luxury, custom-made shades with fine Italian silk, by acquiring them you could expand into a new customer base (luxury buyers). Likewise, if there is a company that offers budget window shades, by acquiring that business you could expand down-market.

## Acquisition Wheel Category Two: When You Want More Leads

In order to get new sales, you usually need new leads. You need more people to whom you can offer your products and services. If you're looking for leads, the best thing to do is acquire media. A whole lot of people have aggregated lists of customers who fit into target markets.

For example, at one company I own, we sell pet supplies for owners of large sporting dogs. Toys, brushes, training materials, treats—you name it. In order to get leads, we decided to look for media platforms that had aggregated large numbers of people in our target audience. We looked for a Facebook group for owners of German shepherds, a YouTube channel with training tips for sporting dogs, a blog for owners of new puppies, and an email list for owners of "large-breed dogs." Our team also found a podcast about the joys of owning golden retrievers, a radio show about dog-training events, a website filled with content about large-breed dogs, and even a LinkedIn group about dog ownership. The list could go on and on.

The owners of those media platforms had invested time and effort to aggregate customers. Each platform contained information that was relevant to people in the target audiences so they would want to keep coming back again and again. The Facebook group owners of German shepherds had more than 10,000 members. The owners had the eyeballs and attention of a mass of people who were exactly in our target market.

By acquiring the media—whether it's a list or a group or a channel—you acquire all of those leads in the process. And these aren't just cold leads—

instead, they are leads who have already opted in for content in the area or areas that you are trying to reach.

**Types of Media**

There are several categories of media that I look for during acquisitions. Each category has subcategories as well, and each of these represents traffic that you can acquire for growth.

1. **Groups:** Meetup groups, masterminds, networking groups, Slack groups, associations

2. **Social Media:** Any social media pages or accounts on X, Instagram, LinkedIn, Facebook, Pinterest; also YouTube channels, LinkedIn groups, Facebook groups

3. **SEO Pages:** Any website or page that ranks on SEO for the keywords you want to rank for. This includes blogs, vlogs, websites, e-commerce sites, guides

4. **Lists:** Email lists, direct mail lists, phone lists, customer lists, affiliate lists, newsletter subscribers, SOP lists, supplier lists, pixeled audience

5. **Products:** Amazon listings (they have their own traffic and internal SEO), Etsy listings, Shopify stores, eBay stores, Facebook stores, Instagram stores

6. **Events:** Radio show, TV show, intensives, events, syndicated shows, podcasts

7. **IP:** Patents, copyrights, URLs, trade secrets, processes, branDS

It's actually pretty simple to acquire media. Most small- to mid- range media is owned by creators who love to create content but may or may not be exhausted by the pressure of building and maintaining an audience. When I make a fair offer—don't nickel and dime people who have spent years building this media—many jump at the opportunity to be paid for their work.

I would be remiss if I didn't warn you that the worst thing you can do is acquire media and turn it into an advertising tool. I had a friend who acquired a Facebook group that had more than 5,000 active users in his target demographic. He was thrilled, but as soon as he acquired the group, he started posting sales pitches. Within a few months, more than half of the active users left the group. If you acquire media, you need to ensure that the content the users have come to love and enjoy continues to reach them. This is good for you, too—it builds loyalty to your brand and allows you to keep attracting new leads.

**Pro Tip: Acquiring Media for SEO**

The other thing about media is it's often ranked in search engines, and these properties will come up on Google search for keywords you probably want to own. For example, if you own a marketing agency and are hoping to get ranked for marketing services, instead of spending months and thousands of dollars trying to get on the front page, you could acquire a website that comes up high on SEO. It's a win-win because people are already going to that website—hence their SEO ranking—and now you have a bunch of content about marketing, plus your content is already ranked.

**Acquisition Wheel Category Three: When You Want More Infrastructure**

Another reason to acquire a new company is to gain the infrastructure you need to grow. We did this one time at our company DigitalMarketer. We had an idea for a SaaS product that we were really excited about—it not only fit into our own growth strategy but we knew hundreds of other companies would want to use it as well. We had never done any software development before (and honestly, I had no idea how to build a software development team). So we acquired a small SaaS company with a full team—including developers, project managers, and managers—in place. As soon as we acquired them, we had a team that could develop our product. It made what would have been a months-long process fast and painless.

This is called acqui-hiring—essentially acquiring a company to get the talent you need to expand and grow your own business. I've seen this done many times in many ways. A few examples:

- A company that was growing rapidly through paid media bought a paid media agency to acquire its buying team.

- A company that had never had a sales force acquired a company with a huge outbound sales team, in addition to an inbound marketing team, and voila: a ready-made sales force.

- A company wanting to install a functional operating system acquired a company with a great operations manager and effective SOPs so it could build a new OS.

- An owner-operated business wanted to add professional management. Instead of hiring a manager, they acquired a company with an amazing management team and went instantly from owner-operated to professionally managed.

You can also do M&A to obtain physical infrastructure. This means another company has the resources you need for growth. Some examples are:

- A manufacturing company that wanted to double their product output acquired another manufacturing company to get access to their machines and factories.

- A marketing company wanted a better email tool, so they bought an email CRM and then expanded the tool to include their preferred features.

- An e-commerce business looking to open a brick-and-mortar storefront acquired a company that had a storefront in a prime location. They sold both the original company's products and theirs in the store.

Whatever talent and resources you need, you may be surprised to find out that it's often easier and faster, and sometimes even less expensive, to acquire it through *acqui-hiring* M&A rather than traditional routes like purchasing and hiring.

- **BDA Products:** BDA stands for before, during, and after products. Parents who buy baby rockers are likely to need maternity clothes and pregnancy products *before* they need the baby rocker. Then at the *same time* they need the baby rocker, they would need a mobile or crib bedding or a baby monitor. *After* they need the baby rocker, they might need a walker or a saucer toy.

- **Upsells:** Maybe you decide to manufacture and sell a premium baby rocker with a digital control panel that includes four positions.

- **Downsells:** Perhaps you know some of your customers can't buy a baby rocker, but maybe they will need a swaddle and some baby blankets.

- **Cross-Sells:** People who need a baby rocker probably also need a baby monitor, or some blankets, or a book about sleep training, or a sleep training service.

- **Bundles:** You could bundle the baby rocker with a cover, some all-natural upholstery cleaner, a mobile for hanging above the rocker, and a breastfeeding pillow.

All of the above options are ways to increase the number of products that your customers buy from you, or the price of the products that they order from you. Spend some time thinking about how you can add any or all of those options to your orders.

These strategies work for more than just physical products. SaaS companies have gotten really good at this—instead of selling software for a one-time fee, they offer tech enablement, support services, and marketing services that help the price to go up.

To do M&A to increase average order value, start by thinking of the products or services you could add to your current orders to increase them. Then think about the companies that are offering those products and services. You can acquire those companies—or parts of them—and, in doing so, increase your AOV and profits at the same time.

**Acquisition Wheel Category Five: When You Want to Increase Your Lifetime Customer Value (LCV)**

Another way to increase revenue and profits (and thus increase your exit value) is to increase your lifetime customer value or LCV. For this, you need to acquire businesses or entities that have a predictable and recurring stream of revenue.

In step 8 of chapter 3, we talked about creating M(A)RR for your business. Hopefully, you have already done this. Now we're talking about how to acquire M(A)RR to increase your LCV. I'm going to share a series of stories about real businesses that acquired M(A)RR rather than create it themselves. I hope these will inspire you to a similar acquisition.

## Auto-Shipping Dog Food (and the Values of Auto-Renew Services)

A friend of mine started a company that sold natural, refrigerated dog food. She was struggling to make the numbers work. She would make a sale, then people would run out, try other dog foods, etc. So she acquired a company that was successful with auto-shipping pet supplies, and put her dog foods on auto-ship along with several other products. It turned her business completely around.

You can do the same thing with services. At DigitalMarketer, we sold certifications. People would take a deep-dive training on a certain area like social media marketing or paid advertising. Once they had completed the training and the test, they would get a certification. It looked great on their resumes, they would get better jobs, and all was good…until their certifications aged three or four years and companies started realizing that a three-year-old certification in social media is essentially obsolete. Kind of like a three-year-old iPhone.

We realized that we needed to put a time limit on our certifications so that they had value, and because we wanted anyone holding the badge to have the most updated training and information. So we merged with a company that offered continuing education units and put an expiration date on the certifications. Now they had to be renewed every year. Everyone won with this: Our customers won as they got continuing education and the most up-to-date certifications; the businesses hiring our customers won as they got highly trained employees; and finally, we won because the certification renewals came with a fee, providing a source of annual recurring revenue (ARR). It was a better brand experience, a better product—and we made more money.

## How-To Videos and the Value of Membership Services

Think about Sam's Club, Costco, and gyms: They are all based on a membership product or service. If you don't have a membership product or service, consider how you can acquire one.

One idea I've seen used to high success is to acquire media with great training or how-to videos on how to best use your product. Then, sell a membership for ongoing access to this content. You could also acquire or merge with a services organization and include a service or tech support membership on a product you sell. Another membership service idea is entertainment—any channel that requires a membership to access the content is a great way to acquire M(A)RR.

## SaaS Solutions

Software as a Service—SaaS—was at the forefront of the idea of M(A)RR. SaaS companies realized early on that by adding a renewable service with their software they could make more money and increase their lifetime order value.

## New Razors and other Consumables

One great example of this is Dollar Shave Club. The owners knew that people always need to buy and replace razors, so they made them a monthly subscription where the replacement was automatically shipped to the customer. I've also seen this done with things like printer ink and printers.

As far as acquisitions go, this would require looking for a consumable item to go with your non-consumable item. For example, if you sold fancy electric toothbrushes, you could acquire a manufacturer of fancy, all-natural toothpastes. Then, each month you could ship your customers a new toothbrush head and a tube of fancy toothpaste.

## Recurring Products

Recently the idea of subscription boxes has really taken off. Think Blue Apron or Hello Fresh or IPSY or one of the hundreds of others. Each of these automatically ships a new box with new products on a regular basis.

Apple has a subscription service where you get a new iPhone each time one comes out. Even Cadillac and Porsche and Audi have gotten in on the repeating services game—they have a subscription model where people can get a new car every two to three years.

To increase your LCV, think about the products that would complement your product. For example, if you sell protein shakes, you could acquire a company that makes protein bars, beef jerky, or other healthy snacks. Turn it into a box and send it to your customers on a monthly basis.

## Recurring Services

Just like the subscription box model, services can work great as recurring subscriptions. For example, many cleaning services offer one-time cleanings, or cleanings on a bi-monthly basis for a discounted rate. This also goes for things like lawn or garden care, haircuts, tutoring, etc.

When it comes to acquisition, you may want to consider companies that offer services in your area. For example, if you sell a cleaning product, you could acquire a cleaning company and offer a cleaning service that uses your products only.

## Internet of Things (IOT) and Smart Devices

Internet of Things (IOT) is essentially tech-enabled order automation. For example, my wife and I have a fancy dishwasher that tracks how many cycles we run and automatically ships rinse aid and dishwasher tabs before we run out. I've seen fridges that automatically reorder water filters when they need to be replaced. Recently, I heard of a coffee company that ships tiny scales. Each time the coffee bag on the scale gets low, it auto-ships a new bag of specially selected, curated artisanal coffee.

Each of these ideas can increase your lifetime order value, and if you do it by acquisition, you will add loads of M(A)RR practically overnight.

**Acquisition Wheel Category Six: When You Want to Increase Your Profit Margin**

The next category on the acquisition wheel is about increasing your profit margins. When I'm looking to acquire, I personally don't like to see a profit margin less than 20 percent in all industries. Many buyers will be similar—so if your margins are lower than 15 to 20 percent, you need to increase them before you can exit.

Generally, when companies want to increase their profit margins, their first instinct is to raise prices. This can be good—sometimes you need to raise your prices—but doing so doesn't always increase margins. You might have to spend more to get customers, or customers may drop off. The quickest and often easiest way to increase profit margin is through what we call *vertical integration*. Essentially, you acquire the middle men in your sales process to scoop up that profit.

Let's say you own a company that sells and manufactures bath bombs. To make a bath bomb, you have to buy salts and oils, then you pay someone to turn those ingredients into bath bombs. Next you have a wholesaler who buys your products in bulk, and then distributes them to retailers who sell those bath bombs to consumers. Your products have to be made, sold to a wholesaler, and placed in stores. Each of those entities takes money from the final margin. If you acquire the ingredient creators, the manufacturing company, the wholesaler, or the retailer, you essentially acquire all the profit that person or company is making.

You could buy a company that makes Epsom salts. Or essential oils. You could acquire the manufacturing equipment. You could buy the wholesaler or find a way to sell direct to retail. You could buy the retailer. Any or all of these will add margin to your business. You will make more money selling the same product.

This works for services as well. Let's say you own a digital marketing agency. You are great at social media marketing so you do all of that in-house, but you don't have much experience with paid media or SEO, so you subcontract a paid media agency and an SEO agency to provide those services for your customers. If you could acquire the other agencies—or their staff—you could cut out the middleman and add that profit to your company.

This can also work for affiliates. Many customers rely on affiliates to sell their products. By acquiring an affiliate network, you again eliminate the middleman and add the money you would pay them to your bottom line.

By acquiring any entity on your supply and distribution chain, you add a huge profit for your business. I heard one story about a business who was paying 2 times ingredients to their manufacturer, then 4 times price to their wholesaler, and then the retailer was selling the product for 6 times price. When it came out, the product was being sold for 48 times ingredient price. By acquiring those entities, all of those 48 times profit went to the original owner of the company. Supply chains often represent leaking margin, so any acquisition that shores that up may mean a huge increase in profits.

**Acquisition Wheel Category Seven: When You Want To Innovate**

The final cog on our Acquisition Wheel is for when you want to innovate. Oftentimes this is done when your products or services are becoming obsolete or dated. If you are a digital marketing agency but you haven't done paid media training since Myspace was a thing, you may want to acquire an experience paid media agency to help you to innovate.

If you need new products or services to bring new life into your company, then this is the category for you to focus on. Oftentimes in this category, you are not acquiring a product or service as much as acquiring the intellectual property behind a product or service that will, in turn, add value to your brand. Some examples of this:

1.  **Patents:** If someone has a patent on a product that you believe would enhance your products or services, then you can obtain that patent. Oftentimes you can then upgrade your product to make it more effective or efficient, and then alert your customers that your product got an upgrade.

2.  **Trademarks:** Author and motivational speaker Tai Lopez specializes in acquiring the trademarks of zombie brands—big brands that have gone out of business or are close to it. For example, he acquired Radio Shack, Dress Barn, and Pier 1 Imports. All three of those brands have gone out of business, but all three remain very recognizable as far as logo and products. By acquiring the trademarks, Lopez is able to put those logos on products he sells. He can put the Radio Shack logo on various MP3 players or the Pier 1 logo on a line of throw pillows. Now those products have the backing of major brands, even though they aren't manufactured or sold by those brands.

3. **Franchises:** Acquire a franchise where you can sell or place your products.

4. **Research labs:** Interesting fact: Apple didn't invent the apple processing system. Apple went to Park (a Xerox facility) and acquired their technology to build the apple processing system.[29] If you know of a lab or research entity that has done the work in your industry that you need to make your products great, acquire it.

5. **Prototypes:** Trade names, logos, brands, and other branding materials can be helpful in making your brand.

This is the most overlooked area, but I have found that by adding new life to your products through innovation, profits tend to rise quickly.

**How to Use the Acquisition Wheel**

I just shared a lot of information with you. Before I finish this section, I want to make sure I'm super clear about how to use it. This is a simple tool, but a very valuable one that can increase your exit price significantly. Here's how:

**Step 1:** Look at your business, your financials, and your struggles and figure out which "problems" you want to solve, or goals you want to meet. You definitely shouldn't try to use Micro M&A to solve every problem, but if you can find one or two or even three categories, it can make a big impact.

**Step 2:** Once you've figured out what you want to solve, figure out which categories in that area would be most effective for you. For example, if you're solving for leads, which types of media work best? If you're solving for innovation, what types of intellectual property do you need?

**Step 3:** Identify companies that fit that category. If you decide you want to acquire control of Facebook groups for pet owners, you should find as many groups that fit your needs as you can. Note: This list can be long.

**Step 4:** Narrow down and rank your list. Once you have a list of potential acquisitions, hone it to your top five to ten and then rank those in order of your top choices and down.

**Step 5:** Approach those top companies and start discussing mergers and acquisitions. If the first one says no, move on to the next.

If you do this once a quarter or even once a year, you will always be in the Micro M&A process, and you will always have M&As helping you solve your problems and reach your goals.

**A Final Comment on Micro M&A**

As I said before, Micro M&A is my thing. I believe mergers and acquisitions are not only some of the most powerful tools any business owner can have, but they can lead to rapid growth for any company.

I was only able to brush the surface in this book, but if you would like to take a deeper dive into this topic, I have more tools. I would love to invite you to join me in learning more, for your current business that you're working to exit, or for any future businesses.

You'll find trainings, case studies, and details on my mastermind (Epic Board) at epicnetwork.com, where M&A operators share how they find, structure, and close deals.

Either way, don't skip this step while you're in the process of exiting. I believe it is one of the most powerful ways you can get Exit-Ready. Even acquiring the tiniest of companies—a list, the rights to a Facebook group, or a patent—can multiply your profits. Micro acquisitions can be a huge boon to any business.

## *Part*
# Three

# ACTUALLY MAKING YOUR EXIT

CHAPTER 6

# PLANNING YOUR EXIT

As you've certainly gathered in the last several chapters, an exit doesn't happen overnight. A lot has to happen between the time you decide you're ready to exit and the time the deal closes. Marketing, preparing the business, identifying buyers, due diligence . . . and the list goes on. These things can occur somewhat quickly for some businesses, especially when the owner is Exit-Ready before they start the process. But as a general rule, becoming Exit-Ready can take a year or more.

By now you also know that I can say with confidence: Owners who plan their exit in advance will get a significantly higher price on the sale than owners who don't. Because of this, I recommend you start the exit process two or three years before you want to sell. This gives you time to prepare your business, go through all eighteen steps, and make sure you have done everything possible to get the most for your business.

In this chapter, I'm going to walk you through the timing for planning your exit. Along the way you'll discover what you need to do at each phase. This chapter will read like a series of to-do lists, but hopefully it will help you organize your thinking so that you have a real, strategic plan as you begin the exit process.

# Nine Things To Do Two to Three Years Before You Exit

Even if you're not in full-on exit mode, you can start taking small steps toward your exit two or even three years in advance. The eighteen steps I shared earlier in this book can all be started long before you actually plan to exit. I often recommend that owners continuously do those tasks to stay Exit-Ready.

## 1. Make a List of Strategic Buyers

Even if you're months or years away from selling, it's a good idea to have the end buyer in mind. Start thinking about the types of buyers who would benefit from acquiring a company like yours. What does your business do that other players in the industry may need? Are there companies with gaps your company could fill? Does your company provide something in the production or sales or marketing process that would benefit them?

Let's say you manufacture water filters. Many types of companies could benefit from your business. The obvious answer is water filter manufacturing companies who don't have a product like yours, but I challenge you to expand your thought process to other ideas. Perhaps there are wholesaling companies that wholesale all kinds of filters. Or a water filter sales company that wants to cut out the middleman. Or a refrigerator or appliance company eager to bundle products.

Think of any gap your company may fill for another company, and add them to your list. At this point, there is no need to contact these companies or even build a relationship with them. Having them in mind as you start the process will inform you as you prepare to exit.

## 2. Have Your Attorney Do Mock Due Diligence

When you go through the exit process, you will have people pouring through your entire entity, looking at every form, every tax filing, every financial statement. Have your attorney spend some time doing mock due diligence so they can flag anything out of place and you can fix it before you are in the middle of an exit.

### 3. Have Your Accountant Do a Mock Audit

Like your mock due diligence, have your accountant or accounting team audit all of your financial statements for the last two to three years. This will ensure that all of your statements are in order, but it will also give you a good picture of your growth trajectory and the profit you can expect, allowing you to better plan for your future exit.

### 4. Get a Professional Valuation

Having a professional team do a valuation for your company can give you a clear picture of what to expect in the exit process. It also allows you to look at ways to increase your value (and thus exit price) using sales data.

### 5. Get Your Labor in Tip-Top Shape

For most companies, their most expensive and valuable assets are the people. Your human resources are also your riskiest assets—they can leave, and an exit plus new ownership causes a lot of disruption that might prompt some employees to bolt. Before you begin the exit process, make sure all of your labor agreements are in compliance and all employment contracts are accurate.

### 6. Get your Intellectual Property in Shape

Make sure you have an accurate list of all of your patents, trademarks, and intellectual property. Make sure it's all properly registered and filed in the appropriate places. This would also be a good time to spin off any IP that isn't part of the core business and may not be wanted by a buyer into its own entities so you can sell it separately or retain it.

**7. If Possible, Resolve Any Unresolved Legal Issues**

Unresolved and threatened lawsuits or claims add big risk to an acquisition. They are often an unknown threat, and a buyer will be leery to purchase or drop the price if there are outstanding legal claims. Resolve as many outstanding claims and lawsuits as possible before you begin the exit process.

**8. Clean Up Your CAP Table**

Before you begin to exit, you need a clear, concise list of everyone who owns an interest in your company or has a right to own an interest in your company. Make sure all of these interests are clearly represented on the capitalization table so buyers can get a clear picture of who they are going into business with and who they may need to buy out.

**9. Invest in Profit-Making Assets and Capital Expenses Only**

When you're thinking of exiting, it is not the time to introduce risky new product lines or expand your office. While you're in the process of exiting, invest your money into profit-making assets and capital expenses as much as possible. Anything that would reduce your profits, reduces your sales price.

## What To Stop Doing Two to Three Years Before You Exit

While the list of things you need to do as you plan to exit is long, the list of things you need to stop doing is equally voluminous. The items on the list below adversely impact the value of your company and therefore will make it more difficult for you to exit—while costing you tons of money in the process.

1.  **Stop Being the Face of Your Business.** Go back and review step 3 in the eighteen-step process for getting Exit-Ready. If you are the key person in your business, then you will have a hard time exiting. Either the buyer will significantly cut the price they are willing to pay—needing to replace you creates a risk for them—or you will stay on as a consultant. If you stay on, you will essentially become an employee, continuing to do the work you're doing now for your business but with no power and less financial incentive. It won't be worth it. You want to exit, not move into a three-to-five-year contract with the business you just sold.

2.  **Stop Taking Tax Write-Offs.** I know this is hard. I have personally felt the pain of this. As we discussed earlier, entrepreneurs have been told for years that they can write off business expenses as one of the perks of owning their business. This is great, and legal, and absolutely something you should do all the way up until a year or two before you exit. Let's look at the math as to why you need to stop doing this. If you write off $100,000 of business expenses each year, you get a marginal amount of tax savings. For example, if you were in the 50 percent tax bracket, you would get approximately $50,000 in tax savings. But if your business garners a 10 times multiple, that $100,000 in write-offs equals $10 million in additional value for your company when you exit. So as hard as it may be, spend the next two or three years adjusting your expenses so you don't take those tax write-offs.

3.  **Stop Paying Your Personal Expenses from the Business.** This goes hand in hand with the last one, but these expenses come right out of your profits that will be used to calculate your exit price. As we've discussed, you should stop paying for things out of your business, like add-on vacations to business trips, a company car, or childcare. That

money goes back into your profit margin.

4. **Stop Paying Down Debt.** This one is also hard. We are trained as business owners to be fiscally responsible, and that often means doing our best to pay down debt as quickly as possible. I'm not recommending that you stop paying your debts—you definitely don't want to default—but I'm recommending that you continue paying minimum payments and invest any excess cash you have in profitable things instead. So, for example, instead of paying down a business loan, acquire a new entity that can add to your company's value, or spend money on marketing expenses to grow your customer base.

5. **Keep Key Employees in Place.** This is really a "keep doing" rather than a "stop doing." But when you're getting ready to exit, it is not the time to consider layoffs or restructuring. Instead, maintain the status quo and keep key employees in place, doing what they do best.

6. **Keep Key Accounts from Leaving.** Similar to number 5, this is not the time to be "firing" customers, or restructuring accounts, or increasing prices. It's time to keep your clients happy and maintain your client base so that a potential buyer sees a whole lot of stability when they look to buy.

7. **Stop Spending Money on Things You Don't Use.** Does anyone else have a bunch of subscriptions and tools that they rarely (if ever) use? This is the time to do an audit and get rid of things you don't use. A few years ago, we had our accounting department do a full audit on our subscriptions and tools that we didn't use or use much. I am too embarrassed to share how much money we saved every month. Don't cut out important tools, but jettison the ones that simply don't add to your company's profitability.

8. **Stop Telling People You're Exiting.** When you're planning to exit, you should keep it a secret within a very small and select group of people such as the CEO, owners, and CFO. If your employees or your clients find out, they may start to panic and leave. Even if you want to be transparent and open, you need to wait until the process is pretty far along before sharing. After all, it's human nature to fear change.

## Create An Advisory Team

The exit process is obviously complex. There is a lot to know, a lot to do, and a lot to manage. I am a lawyer by trade and have done hundreds of acquisitions and exits in my career. But even with that level of experience, I still use an advisory team for every exit. It allows me to make the best possible decisions and be as prepared as I can to get the most out of every exit and acquisition.

Now is the time for you to build an advisory team. In my experience, the perfect advisory team actually comprises three different teams: an exit team, a planning team, and an operations team. In this section, I'll walk you through who needs to be on each team and how you can help the teams work together to plan a successful exit. Here's how you build your perfect advisory team:

### Team One: The Exit Team

The exit team does all of the hard work for the actual exit. They are the pros who advise you on the actual exit process and perform tasks necessary for you to exit. This team should consist of:

1. **An exit advisor:** This person oversees the exit process and advises you on next steps and how to get the most from your exit. They should be experienced in M&A—possibly an attorney. I do a lot of consulting

work as an exit advisor for owners looking to exit. While this person could be an accountant or attorney, it's important that they are not your personal accountant or attorney. Instead, it needs to be someone with lots of M&A experience who can talk you through practical considerations and guide you and your attorney and accountant in the process.

2.  **An M&A attorney:** Find an attorney who specializes in mergers and acquisitions. This is a highly complex field, and you want an attorney who knows all of the legal intricacies of exits so you can make sure everything is in order. You generally do not need your regular attorney to be involved beyond providing data or corporate legal documents requested by M&A counsel.

3.  **An accountant:** You need an accountant who is able to organize all of your financial statements and make sure everything is in order. Additionally, this person will confer with the buyer to answer any financial questions about your company. This could be your existing accountant.

4.  **A tax attorney:** A tax attorney can advise you on the tax implications of this sale and help you plan your exit so you will be in a tax-advantaged position after you exit. The tax attorney usually coordinates with and reports to the M&A attorney.

5.  **A wealth manager or advisor:** What are you going to do with the money you get from the sale? How will you maintain your standard of income? (Or, *can* you maintain that standard?) A lot of what is paid out from your business will go away when you sell, so a wealth advisor will help you manage your money in ways that allow you to be financially

sound even after you stop getting income from the company.

6.  **An investment banker.** The investment banker runs the sale process for you—they generally find the buyer for you, keep pace with the buyer, guide both parties in the process, and advise everyone on how to make sure the deal moves to completion.

## Team Two: The Planning Team

Next up is the planning team. Some of the members of your exit team (e.g., the exit advisor, the accountant, the attorneys) will be on this team as well. This team helps you with all the planning steps leading up to the exit, and helps you with all of the due diligence to get your documents and records in order. This team will do the following tasks:

1.  **Pre-exit entity structuring:** Make sure your business is structured in a way that is most advantageous for the exit. See step 2 in chapter 5. A good planning advisor will figure out what actual asset or set of assets a potential buyer will want to acquire and then spin off or remove any assets that shouldn't be part of it to give you maximum value.

2.  **Tax and estate planning:** Make sure your taxes are in order and you are able to maintain or grow your estate after you exit.

3.  **Financial diligence:** Audits and paperwork regarding your finances.

4.  **Optimize SDE or EBITDA:** As we discussed in chapters 2 and 3, make sure your profits are as high as they can be leading into the exit.

5.  **Employee contracts and key team retention:** The planning team will make sure your employee contracts are in place and that there is a retention program ready to help key employees stay as management changes.

6. **Legal diligence:** Your legal team needs to get all of your entities, IP documents, and governance documents in place and organized.

7. **Commercial diligence:** Review of NPS score, ops review, SOPs, and org chart.

8. **CapEx and OpEx initiatives:** Any review and organization of your CAP tables and organizational tables to make sure everything is ready and optimized for exit.

9. **Mock due diligence**. As we discussed earlier, I recommend that your planning team do what I call mock due diligence. Have your team do mock commercial due diligence (CDD), financial due diligence (FDD), and legal due diligence (LDD), and plug any holes that could kill your deal or impact the sale price.

**Team Three: The Operations Team**

This team is likely already in place, performing the day-to-day operations of your business. From that group, you do need to select a few key individuals who, on a need-to-know basis, can adjust your operations to plan for your exit. This team will:

1. **Continue operating as normal.** Help the business run seamlessly and continue on the same path without major blips.

2. **Hire and invest as normal,** but avoid extraordinary growth expenses. You don't want a potential buyer to see a steep drop-off in the growth trajectory before they buy, but this isn't the time to invest in huge, risky growth initiatives. If you spend $1 million on a growth initiative that will take two years to realize, that money is essentially lost to you (and the next owner will benefit from it).

3. **Continue existing expansion and growth plans.** That said, any existing expansion and growth plans should continue as planned.

4. **Maintain the confidentiality of the intent to sell until necessary**. I want to be really clear: If you tell your entire staff, it will cause panic. People will leave, get scared, tell others, tell customers, and then customers may leave. It will not go well. Your exit operations team should be small and only include trusted employees who you know will support you without panicking or talking about the exit.

5. **Maximize SDE or EBITDA.** This team should do everything possible to maximize profits in the years before you exit to ensure the best possible exit price. See chapter 4.

## Planning Takes Time

I'm sure you are feeling a bit overwhelmed. Planning takes time and a lot of thought. When you see lists like the ones in this chapter, it's easy to feel like exiting will take forever.

Let me give you a pep talk: The mere fact that you're reading this means you've gotten this far. You're thinking and planning and strategizing. You're taking steps to get ready. You're being thoughtful and strategic. This work isn't for naught. Because of this work, you'll get much more from your exit. Pulling levers to get higher valuation, creating strategies to realize higher profit margins, strategic M&A, careful due diligence, strong audits of your financials, and all of the other work you do is hard work, but it's powerful work. Each of the things I listed in this chapter will help propel your company to a higher valuation, a higher multiple, and a higher price at exit.

CHAPTER 7

# THE RIGHT EXIT PROCESS FOR YOU

Before you start reading this chapter, I'm going to ask you to flip way back to chapter 1, when I described the types of exits that each entrepreneur makes. Remember how I told you that first you exit the line, then the staff, then the org chart, and so on? Well, now that we have gone through all the things you need to do to get ready to exit, let's discuss five *levels of selling*. (Not to be confused with the levels of exiting we've already discussed.)

Do you want to sell nothing or everything? Do you want to keep control of your business to the end, never letting go of even a percentage? Or are you hoping to exit fully and never look back?

The vast majority of owners find themselves somewhere in the middle. They want to sell some of their company—they want the big payday that comes with an exit. They want to move on to the next thing in their lives—but they don't want to get rid of everything. They want to maintain some control, maybe as an advisor or board member, or retain some of their equity, or perhaps keep a division or a patent or intellectual property as they move to a new thing.

There are five levels of sales transactions, each with different pros and cons, and each with different levels of risk and reward. On the coming pages I'm going to walk you through the five levels, the types of transactions, and the exit processes that owners use, so that you can make the best decision for you as you move forward.

## Level One: Do Nothing

This level is exactly what it sounds like: You don't exit. You keep running your business, you maintain 100 percent control. You don't get a payday, but you also don't lose your paycheck. There's no dilution of ownership, no distraction of operations. Everything stays the same.

My guess is that no one who has read this far is looking for a level one outcome. After all, if you don't want to exit, why did you pick up and read a book on being Exit-Ready? That said, there are some real cons to this level as well. When you don't exit, you have no ability to move on, try new things, or retire. You are caught in the day-to-day with all of your eggs in one basket. You won't get a big payday. If you do decide to take distributions on the business, they will be subject to taxes.

## Level Two: Debt Recap

Debt recap involves taking on debt in order to cash out some of the equity you have in the company so you can make a mini-exit and get a small personal payday. There will be a small dilution of warrants to a debt owner. You won't be able to take much cash out; you will need to retain cash to pay the debt or you will lose flexibility in operating your business. Distributions may be capped based on the performance of your company so you are not able to take more money out after the debt recap than you took out before it.

A dept recap won't cause you to lose much control of the company, but you also don't gain much from this level because you don't get much cash out of the deal.

## Level Three: Minority Recap

A minority recap allows you to keep majority control of the company, but there is some dilution as you give up some of your equity. The good news is that this comes with a medium-sized payday as you take chips off the table and cash them in.

A minority recap is also likely to come with some growth capital for your company. Whoever joins you will add some cash to the kitty to help you grow and scale. They also may add some resources like personal connections that will allow the business to scale, giving you a potential second big payday when you exit fully at some point.

The downside of a minority recap is there will be some equity dilution, and you'll be dealing with someone else in the day-to-day operations of your company. You may be attracted or repelled by these new owners and options. Since you lose some control, it can be hard to get used to.

## Level Four: Majority Recap

A majority recap comes with all the bells and whistles you would expect from an exit. You get a big payday, your company gets capital to grow, perhaps some smart money investors will bring additional resources, and you'll potentially even get a second (albeit smaller) payday if the new majority owners decide to exit again after some growth in valuation.

With a majority recap, you lose your majority stake in the company, which means you have minimal control over what happens. Additionally, there is a debt risk because whoever comes in will likely put debt on the company to buy in, which puts your stake at risk. With a majority recap, you will still have some equity, and therefore you maintain some control and retain some decision-making power.

## Level Five: Outright Sale

This is a retire-to-the-beach type of sale. You get a big payday on the full value of your company. You also could get possible additional paydays with earnout caveats. This is great: lots of money, which makes all of the blood, sweat, and tears you poured into your business worth it.

The downside of outright sale is you lose full control. You will no longer have a stake in the business, help determine how to grow it, or get a say on whether they merge, shut it down, restructure—and you cannot protect your team. The new ownership may ask you to stay around for a while as a consultant, but for all intents and purposes, you are done with the business.

I recommend that you spend some time thinking about which of the five levels will best meet your needs. Go back and reread the first four chapters of this book and consider your company, your exit, your number, and more. None of the above are "wrong" in any way—but some may fit your needs better than others.

## Which Exit Transaction is Right For You?

Now that you've decided what level of sale you want to make, it's time to actually make that sale. As I'm sure you've realized by now, buying a business is nothing like buying a new shirt at Nordstrom or a new car at the Tesla dealership. It's much more complex than even big real estate transactions. It takes time and patience and a lot of thought.

The added complexity means there isn't just one type of transaction; there are four types, each with their own set of rules, pros, and cons.

### Transaction #1: The Buyer Approaches You

Time and time again, I see exits happen when a buyer approaches the owner and asks if they want to sell. The owner wasn't necessarily thinking of exiting, but upon seeing the offer, they sell. Transaction done. Exit complete. Check, check, and check.

I admit: I often approach owners to see if they want to sell. If I see a business (or a media property or a division of a company) that I think would strategically help my own business, I contact the owner. Why not? It's a great way to do M&A and it eliminates months of time from the process. Plus, I can usually get a great deal this way.

When you're on the selling side, there are some pros and cons to a buyer-initiated exit. I'm not saying it's always a bad thing to do—like I said, I often do it—but there are things to consider.

### Pros to a Buyer-Initiated Transaction

- **Fast-moving.** When a buyer approaches you to buy your business, you can be assured that the process will move quickly. You won't have to do any of the marketing to find a buyer, or go through any of the process of figuring out which buyer to choose.

- **Little distraction.** Making an exit takes a lot of time and effort. It also has a tendency to disrupt the operations of your business. The less focus you are putting into finding a buyer, the more you can put into growing your business and keeping operations on track.

- **Confidentiality.** News of a potential sale leaking out can cause chaos in your operations. People freak out and leave. Customers panic. It's bad. Oftentimes the buying process is full of NDAs and hushed conversations. If you have a single buyer who approached you, the issue of confidentiality is much more controlled. If anything leaks, you know who leaked it—and they have a lot of motivation not to leak the sale; it would hurt them as much as it hurts you.

**Cons to a Buyer-Initiated Transaction:**

- **No challenge means a lower price.** The current M&A climate allows for many buyers to reach out to owners and initiate strategic acquisitions because they know they will pay more if the business goes to auction. If there isn't competition to buy your business—if there is only one buyer at the table—then the price will be lower. There's no marketing, no choice, no bidding.

- **Weak negotiating position.** When no one else is bidding on the business, you are in a weak position. You can't leverage offers or ask for any special provisions.

- **The process can drag on.** With no other suitors at the table, the buyer has no incentive to move the sale along. They can drag it out as long as they want, and as a general rule, when things drag on, it's never good for the seller.

- **Distraction to operations.** I know I wrote buyer-initiated transactions have less distraction to operations in the pros section—and that's true. When you don't have to go out and find a buyer and take bids or go to auction, there is less distraction. However, as noted just above, if the sales process drags on and on, it becomes a big distraction. That's why this is both a pro and a con to this type of transaction.

## Transaction #2: You Target and Approach Buyers One-on-One

In this type of transaction, you as the seller have come up with a list of targets that you think would be good strategic buyers. (Creating this list is number one on the list of Nine Things to Do Two to Three Years Before You Exit in chapter 6.) Once you have the list, you approach them one-on-one to ask about a sale, starting with the best option for you.

## Pros to a Targeted One-on-One Transaction

- **You control the process.** You found the right buyer, you initiated contact, and therefore, you control the process. The timing is in your hands, the next steps are in your hands, and the buyer is your choice.

- **Limited distraction.** Similar to a buyer-initiated transaction, when you target and approach a buyer one-on-one, there is limited distraction to your operations as there is no marketing. There also won't be groups upon groups coming in to see the operations of your business or talk to your managers.

- **Confidentiality.** Again, with one buyer, there is much less risk that your private financial and operations details will be leaked.

- **High-quality buyer.** You chose the buyer you were going to approach, so you likely picked someone who aligned with you and your vision for the business. You know the buyer is not only someone who will strategically benefit your business, but also someone who has the funds to make the transaction happen.

### Cons to a Targeted One-on-One Transaction

- **Lower sales price.** When you approach the buyer, you may end up with a slightly higher sales price than if the buyer approaches you, but there is still no real competition for the sale, so the price you get will be lower than it could be.

- **The sale could drag on.** Just like in a buyer-initiated sale, when there is no competition, there is little incentive for the buyer to get the sale closed quickly, so it can take more time, which can be a distraction to operations and delay your payday.

### Transaction #3: You Target and Approach a Buyer Group

Now we are getting to my favorite types of transactions. I want to be clear (and we'll talk about this more in a bit) that these last two transactions carry a potential for a higher exit price, but they also pose a higher risk. I tend to gravitate toward the higher-risk, higher-reward transaction types, but you need to spend some time weighing which option is best for you.

In this type of transaction, the seller approaches several targeted buyers on their list and lets them know the business is for sale. From there, each of those businesses has a chance to see the data room, perform due diligence, walk through the process—and then a final buyer is selected.

## Pros to a Buyer-Group Transaction

- **Higher price.** From the very beginning, the buyers know that they are in competition with others to get the business. This means that the buyers will compete to make the best offer possible.

- **You own control of the process.** Just like when you approach one buyer, when you approach a group of buyers, you control the process. You decide when to approach, who to approach, and when to start moving through the process.

- **High-quality buyers.** Since you choose the buyers, you can be assured they are high-quality and strategically aligned to your vision. If you have three or four or five equally strategic buyers on your list, this type of transaction is a great way to drive the price up while ensuring that you have a great buyer in the end.

- **You choose the buyer.** You can choose the buyer that meets your needs strategically—even if they aren't the highest bid.

## Cons to a Buyer-Group Transaction

- **Fewer potential buyers than an auction.** With strategically selected buyers, you have fewer potential buyers than you would if you went to auction. This will likely mean a lower price than you could potentially get at auction, although the price for this type of transaction is still much higher than a single-buyer transaction.

- **Risk of your confidential data leaking.** The more people who see your confidential financial and product information, the more chance there is of a leak. When there are multiple buyers, it's hard to determine who made the leak and when.

- **Your employees and customers have a good chance of finding out.** With multiple businesses looking at your stuff and talking to your teams, it's likely employees and even customers will find out you're selling, which could result in disruption and people leaving.

- **High level of disruption to operations.** There will be multiple buyers meeting with your management team, looking at your assets, and observing operations. This leads to a lot of disruption and can cause significant loss of productivity.

## Transaction #4: Take Your Business to Market in an Auction Transaction

The final type of transaction has a lot of risk…and potentially a lot of reward. For this type, you take your business to market in an auction. Any potential buyers who want to bid on it, can. The highest bid wins the prize.

### Pros to an Auction Transaction

- **Premium price.** When there are multiple interested parties bidding on your business, you'll get the highest possible price.

- **Fast-moving.** Auction transactions are fast. I've seen them close as quickly as a few weeks, although they generally take between sixty to ninety days. Still, if you want to sell fast, an auction can take a fraction of the time that some of the other transactions take.

- **Maximum competition among buyers.** In addition to driving the price up, competition among buyers means you can ask for terms and provisions, and companies will be likely to give them to you as they compete for the winning bid.

### Cons to an Auction Transaction

- **Huge distraction to operations.** Several potential buyers means there will be a stream of people digging around in your data room, coming to meet with your management, and searching through all of your stuff. You will have visits to your offices, meetings with multiple teams, and generally lots of people spending lots of time working to make this transaction happen.

- **Big risk of data leaking.** When multiple buyers are looking at your data room, lots of people can see your confidential information. If there is a leak, you likely won't know its source, and you won't be able to contain it.

- **Your employees and customers will likely know.** There are no secrets kept when your business goes to auction. It is likely that your customers and employees will find out fairly quickly, which could result in people choosing to leave rather than face the risk of upcoming changes.

- **Your competitors may get access to your information.** I've heard of situations where competitors joined a bidding process at auction solely to gain access to a company's financial and product information. Having an auction process exposes your confidential information to competitors.

- **The highest bidder wins**. Yes, you'll get a high price, but some other negotiable things like spinning off divisions or retaining intellectual property may be out of your control. Additionally, you may not be able to make requests like retaining your teams, keeping management in place, and so on.

## How Do You Know Which Transaction to Choose?

So how do you know which exit transaction is right for you? I like to think of picking an exit transaction as an inverse reaction based on your risk tolerance. The least risky transaction comes with the lowest price. Then, as the level of risk goes up, so does your price.

Transaction type 1—where a buyer approaches you—comes with minimal risk. It is unlikely that your confidential information will get leaked, that your management team will have their operations taken over by a buyer, or that your employees and customers will find out your business is for sale.

That all sounds good, right? But with that type of transaction, you are likely to get a much lower price than you would with riskier transactions, and you might spend a long time waiting as the process drags on and on.

Then, as you choose risker transactions—maybe you approach a group of buyers (type 3) or consider auction (type 4)—you gain yourself a likelihood of a higher price, and the process will likely move more quickly, but you risk leaking of your confidential information and that more people will know about your potential sale.

As you consider the type of transaction you want to make, consider your risk tolerance. I mentioned earlier that I often choose to take some risks to garner a higher sales price—I am drawn to transaction types 3 and 4. I am willing to risk possible confidential information being leaked, or my employees or teams finding out about the transaction. I'm also willing to risk some (temporary) disruption to operations if it means I can get a higher exit price for the business.

But not every business owner is willing to take those risks, and that's okay. Maybe you know there is a competitor who would do anything to take you down. Maybe you want to keep your teams intact and maintain some control of the business. Maybe you want to choose the right strategic buyer for you. Or you're worried your teams will sniff out a potential exit and melt into chaos. Or maybe you're okay with a long, slow, drawn-out process. These are all good reasons to stay with a less risky transaction. The important thing is that you consider your options and choose the option that you think best fits your needs.

CHAPTER 8

# FINDING A BUYER FOR YOUR BUSINESS

Max and Renee met while they both worked in the construction industry. It didn't take long for them to realize they had very complementary skills and would make a great team if they started a business together. They did just that, and six years later they owned one of the largest solar companies in the Midwestern United States.

When they came to me, their interests had turned from solar installations to real estate investing. They were also ready to pursue their next adventures individually as opposed to together. They were still friends; they just had different goals, desires, and directions they wanted to go. It was time to see how they could cash in on their success over the past several years and what kind of payday that might generate.

We gathered all the data they would need to create a "data room" for prospective buyers to review once they had been qualified and signed a nondisclosure agreement. As discussed earlier, a data room is just a fancy term for a folder on a secure, password-protected server that allows access to documents with critical information about the business. The data room also monitors who, when, and what documents were accessed by potential buyers.

Over the next several months, we assembled the team: a mergers and acquisitions attorney, their existing accounting firm, a tax attorney, an investment banker, and me as acquisitions advisor and negotiator.

Initially, they hoped to sell the business for $100 million. Once we got into it, researched all of the likely ideal buyers, conducted our outreach, went through extensive negotiations, and remained patient during the roughly fourteen months it took to do all of that, we settled on an exit valuation of $220 million, more than double the initial goal.

Approaching your exit in a strategic, measured fashion with the right team of professionals, the right strategy, patience, the right timing, and clear goals, can literally mean the difference between an "okay" exit and an absolutely stellar one.

That's why I caution against running to get advice from people you know who have made an exit, without knowing the full experience. What was the process they went through leading to the exit? What was the initial offer compared to the final number? How did the deal get structured to provide the greatest net cash to the seller vis-a-vis taxes and terms? What did the noncompete agreements look like? All these questions and many more need answered to determine whether the person now presenting themselves as an accomplished exit engineer actually has the chops to help you get and keep the most when you decide to sell your company, and to get you the best terms for life after the exit.

Once you have decided that you're going to sell, it's time to start looking for the right buyer for your business. In some cases, your buyers will come to you, as you have seen from many of the examples I've provided throughout this book.

But in the vast majority of transactions, the selling company identifies prospective buyers and approaches them. This is one of the times when you will need to engage a professional team to help you. Not only is finding a buyer daunting and time-consuming, but if you don't know what to look for or where to look, you have a good chance of failing to identify motivated buyers for your outreach list, or of finding a buyer that's not a great fit. Both missteps will result in a lower sales price, less attractive terms, or a less-than-strategic exit.

The exit advisory team you assemble to help you is a great place to start. As discussed in chapter 6 under "Create an Advisory Team," your first pick should be an exit advisor. This is someone who has been there, seen that, and been involved in at least one hundred transactions. I realize that may sound like a lot of experience for a minimum, but the truth is that there are so many different permutations of exits that unless someone has gone through at least one hundred, they are likely to be missing experience that, at some point during the exit process, will be critical to you achieving the best exit for you and your business.

Start with the exit advisor because they can help you evaluate your current legal counsel and accounting team to determine whether and to what degree they should be involved in the process. A skilled and experienced exit advisor will also help you fill the gaps in your current advisors and retain the experts that will ensure you achieve your most ideal exit.

The rest of your team will likely include a mergers and acquisitions attorney, an investment banker, a financial advisor, and an accountant. Another great reason to have a team that is deep in M&A experience is that people on that team will likely know many potential buyers. They also know how to run an exit process and navigate an environment with multiple bidders, all while working together as a coherent team. They know how to negotiate key terms and get the price you want.

I can promise you that if you choose your exit advisory team wisely, and following some of the recommendations I make in this chapter, you will find the right buyer for your business and exit at the best price and with the best terms.

## How to Source a Buyer

Even with your Exit Advisory Team in place, you'll still have to do some of the legwork to find the right buyer. After all, you know your company better than anyone else, and you're the one who understands why you want to sell and who your ideal buyer is. After that, you can hand the research and work over to your advisory team to finish the process.

With Max and Renee, we spent several months identifying ideal buyers before we began our comprehensive outreach plan.

Here are the first steps in sourcing a buyer:

**Step One: Make a list of direct competitors.**

Spend some time (if possible, with a few members of your trusted management team) writing a list of your direct competitors. Think about the companies that are always fighting you for market share, and put them at the top of your list.

Direct competitors are frequently buyers because acquiring a competitor increases one's market share substantially. Quite a few merger synergies can be achieved instantly by acquiring a competitor. Merger synergies, by the way, are simply the benefits of merging two similar companies together.

For example: a shared executive team, shared service fleets, shared support resources (finance, HR, customer service), cross-selling opportunities, and so on.

We received an offer that led to the sale of one of our event companies because a direct competitor reached out to us directly. Recently, we received an offer from a direct competitor to one of our professional business services companies. Direct outreach to competitors is one of the most productive types of outreach when building your potential buyer list.

**Step Two: Make a list of indirect competitors.**

Once you have your list of direct competitors, start thinking about your indirect competitors. Consider companies that have a similar website, close URLs, or comparable keyword traffic. Also, consider companies with similar products that are sold in a different geographical market, as well as companies with products that would be an upsell or downsell to your product.

When we were looking to add services our clients were asking for in one of our service companies, we made a list of our indirect competitors that provided those services. We then began reaching out and ended up acquiring one of those competitors. When we wanted to sell our printing company, we reached out to our biggest referral sources that were sending us business and suggested that they consider acquiring the printing company to capture those profits in-house instead of referring the business and associated profits out of their company. In both cases the result was a win-win, and it can be for you as well.

**Step Three: Research Potential Private Equity Firms**

Ask your Exit Advisory Team to do some research into private equity funds that acquire businesses like yours. Start with websites like Crunchbase.com,

Pitchbook.com, or PrivateEquityInfo.com.

One of my clients had a large portfolio of agribusinesses to sell. I helped conduct a comprehensive search of funds that specialized in the agricultural industry. We were ultimately able to identify multiple buyers that eventually led to a successful sale.

**Step Four: Research Other Potential Companies**

In addition to researching private equity firms, I would research family offices and other businesses that invest in businesses like yours. Family offices are generally funded from a single person or family member to manage the investments of that person or family. Think of them like a private equity fund, but with only a single investor. The best sources for information on family offices, their contact information, and investment preferences are FamilyOfficeList.org or FamilyOffices.com.

Once you've done all of this research, add the results from each of the above categories to one giant list. This is your target list of potential buyers for your business. It can be long—it may have ten, twenty, fifty, or even one hundred names on it. It's good to spread your net wide and give yourself lots of options. For Max and Renee's business, we had a list of more than one hundred potential buyers.

## You Have Your List, What's Next?

Before you reach out and make an inquiry, you want to make sure the potential buyers on your list would be a good fit. There are two main reasons that people buy businesses: strategy and finances.

A *strategic buyer* wants to buy your business to further promote their own strategy. Your business fills a gap for them. You may have a product they want to add to their product line, or a storefront that's just right for their growth plan, or a team that they need for their sales goals. Strategic buyers buy to get market expansion, product expansion, or new capabilities. Whatever it is, this type of buyer thinks your business would fit into their business strategy. This is a value play to enhance their overall strategic mission.

We once acquired a tax preparation business as a strategic acquisition to complement our entity formation business. We then acquired a corporate credit-building software company and are in the process of acquiring a law firm too—all as strategic acquisitions.

In a few other cases, we: sold one of our content creation businesses to a pharmaceutical company that needed to acqui-hire an entire team of content creators to boost its bottom line; acquired a lab for one of our supplement marketing businesses; and sold a niche software company that we owned to a larger software company that wanted to integrate it into its existing suite of software products.

Similarly, I helped a client sell part of his business to a large software company that wanted access to his clients. We sold a blog specializing in niche content to a company that sold products and services to the audience that we had aggregated. And we sold a retail store to an online website that wanted to have a physical store presence.

Strategic deals abound and are a rich source of buyers who often see substantially more value in these acquisitions than financial buyers would see, because the acquisition fills some gap in their product or service range or connects their existing customers to products or services that those customers are already purchasing from someone else.

On the other hand, financial buyers are simply looking to earn money from your business. Maybe they see your growth potential or have seen companies in your industry earn a lot of money. These buyers acquire businesses, invest in them, scale them, and often sell them. They look almost exclusively at financial performance, and are hoping for a big return on their investment.

Consider your list of potential buyers. Which businesses fall into which categories? It's likely that your competitors are potential strategic buyers, whereas the private equity firms are financial buyers. It's possible that some of the businesses on your list will fall into both categories, but the vast majority will fit into one or the other. The next step is to break your list into two lists—one for strategic buyers and one for financial buyers.

## Which Type of Buyer is Better?

For obvious reasons, there is no single answer to this question. I've sold companies to both strategic buyers and to financial buyers, and I have bought businesses for both strategic reasons and financial reasons. What's best for you as you exit depends on a variety of factors. Let's discuss the advantages and disadvantages to each type of buyer.

### Advantages to Selling to a Strategic Buyer

We now know that a strategic buyer is acquiring your company not just for financial reasons, but because your company will bring them value beyond money. For similar reasons that you may have acquired a company through Micro M&A, these buyers may be looking to acquire your business. Your company likely fills a gap they need to fill to make their company better, or solves a problem that they've been trying to solve. Because of this, there are some real advantages to selling to a strategic buyer:

- **Highest sales price.** A strategic buyer is willing to pay more because your company brings them value beyond just a financial transaction.

- **A skilled partner.** A strategic buyer has some skill in your industry. This means your company will have a new skilled owner to help it grow and succeed. This is especially advantageous if you're not making a full 100 percent exit—if you get a skilled partner, you can be assured that in the coming years, your company will grow and scale and reach its objectives.

- **Merger synergies.** There are potential synergies to reduce costs that come with a merger. For example, if both companies are manufacturing products on the same or similar machinery, they could combine manufacturing capabilities and sell off half of their machines. You can also combine other duplicated resources like office space, marketing lists, and even human resources. Still, I have found that merger synergies often don't pan out as expected. In fact, I've rarely seen them result in much impact. There is sometimes a small savings, but it's often not as valuable as it appears to be. Research bears this out as well. One study concluded that 56 percent of mergers and acquisitions fail to realize the intended benefits.[1] This often happens because investment bankers and other parties involved overestimate the benefits of the merger or acquisition, or unanticipated issues arise when integrating the acquired company into the acquiring company. It can also happen because debt service

1 Mohd Abdul Moid Siddiqui, Ayesha Farooq, "Mergers and Acquisitions: Failures and Causes, an Evidence-based Approach," *International Journal of Interdisciplinary Research and Innovations*, Vol. 7, Issue 2 (2019), 147–152, https://www.researchpublish.com/upload/book/Mergers%20and%20Acquisitions-7402.pdf.

exceeds the combined companies' ability to pay it, or if cultural issues between the two companies are stark and cannot be bridged.

- **Access to best practices.** Interestingly, something I've found very valuable when two companies merge is that both are able to combine their insight about what works best in their market. They receive access to each other's best practices. This often smooths out operations hiccups and creates an opportunity for both companies to improve systems and processes.

- **Potential improved management.** With an acquisition—especially if a larger company takes over a smaller one—the larger business is able to bring in new management that is often more experienced. This leadership results in new processes and upgraded operating systems. On the flip side, a smaller, more entrepreneurial company may come with managers that have new ideas that can benefit the larger company as well.

- **Additional resources.** Anytime two companies merge, their resources combine. This means a new resource pool that can fill gaps and streamline productivity. For example, if you merge two sales teams, perhaps some of the salespeople who work certain territories can combine forces, or take on new territories and expand.

- **Increased market share.** With a strategic merger of two companies, the combined market share increases. With more products to sell, more leads to follow, more customers to serve, the market share gets much bigger.

- **Potential to reduce competition.** As your market share increases, the market share of your competitors decreases.

### Disadvantages to Selling to a Strategic Buyer

There are some disadvantages to selling to a strategic buyer as well. Because this buyer has an interest in your company to fill a strategic gap, they want your company as it is, complete. This carries a number of implications:

- **Loss of control of the direction of the company.** If you sell your company to a strategic buyer, that buyer will gain at least some if not all control. They likely understand the industry and have their own strategic vision. With this in mind, it's important to be sure you are on the same page about who will have what roles, who will report to whom, and how much control they will have over various aspects of the business. Plus, you'll need to be on the same page about the vision of the combined enterprise after the merger as you go through the sales process.

- **Potential shift in existing company culture.** If you merge two companies, there will always be a shift in company culture. Sometimes that shift is for the better; other times, it makes things hard and employees start to leave. Make sure to get a good handle on the culture of a company that is acquiring yours before you sell, or you risk losing a lot of good employees.

- **Clashes with new management or team members.** As part of the same shift noted above, the clash of cultures between two companies almost always results in people being upset and leaving—or staying but not being happy about it. With any strategic purchase, there is a potential for skirmishes as two teams become one.

- **Customer concerns resulting in loss of sales.** New systems, new employees, new teams, and new management can all result in customers leaving.

- **Integration challenges.** Any time two companies merge, they have to integrate. This can get challenging. For example, let's say Company A uses one vendor management system and Company B uses another. Issues are bound to surface that could result in lost vendors or sales as Company B learns to use the new system and transitions all of their vendors to it.

- **Required employment contracts.** A merger often requires new employment contracts to be written. If a smaller company is absorbed by a larger one, those contracts are often longer and more onerous.

- **Your confidential information could be known by competitors.** If you open up your sale to multiple buyers, and those buyers are all strategic buyers, that means that even if you close the sale with one, other companies who are likely competitors will now know your confidential financial information.

- **Noncompete agreements.** Most large companies will require noncompete agreements from your employees, especially senior managers. This can be frustrating to many as transition often incentivizes people to look for new jobs.

- **Minimal opportunities for a second payday.** A strategic buyer wants to integrate your business into theirs and use it to add value to their business. This means it's highly unlikely, even if you retain some equity, that you will get a second payday.

While all of these disadvantages are real, if you decide ahead of time which exit level is right for you, you can face these headwinds head-on. The disadvantages won't disappear, but you'll know what you're getting into and can prepare accordingly.

## Advantages to Selling to a Financial Buyer

A financial buyer often leads to a much simpler sales process. They aren't worried about how your operating systems are functioning, or how your products are manufactured. Instead, they just want to know the bottom line. This has some strong advantages:

- **Fair sales price.** While the sales price likely won't be as high as with a strategic buyer, financial buyers are generally willing to spend a fair amount and give you what your company is worth.

- **Experienced, prestigious board.** Generally, financial buyers come with a seasoned, high-quality board of directors who will take over your company and run it with precision. This can be especially good for a company that is newer or smaller.

- **Savvy senior management.** Similarly, experienced senior managers will often step in after a financial buyer acquires a business, giving the company a savvy team to help them grow.

- **Skilled financial partner.** Financial buyers are often skilled at— you guessed it—finances. They know how to manage money and how to grow the value of a company. A financial buyer can come in and transform the value of your business.

- **Access to growth capital.** Because they are basing their purchase on the potential ROI, financial buyers will often sink growth capital into a company that they acquire to help it flourish. This is a great opportunity to scale your company and see it reach all of its objectives. It can be especially appealing if you retain some equity or other financial stake in the company.

- **Potential incentives for current management.** A financial buyer will often incentivize your existing team to reach growth objectives.

This means when they meet certain milestones, they will have access to bonuses and other incentives.

- **Opportunity for second payday.** If you retain a portion of your equity and the new buyer grows, scales, and flips your company, you have the potential for a large second payday when they resell the company. This is an option when you sell less than 100 percent of your company to a buyer, which is frequently the preferred structure for most buyers, both strategic and financial. Typically, they will acquire 70 to 90 percent of your company in the initial buy while you retain the remaining 10 to 30 percent. They will then grow the company and sell it for 5 to 10 times more than they purchased it from you. If that happens, your 10 to 30 percent can often be worth more in that second sale than the percentage you sold in the first transaction. This is often referred to as "the second bite at the apple."

- **Ability to spin out entities or IP**. A financial buyer wants to buy your company, grow it, and then resell it. With this in mind, some of your intellectual property like logos or patents or even some entire divisions may not interest them. Step 4 on the list of eighteen steps to being Exit-Ready will prepare you for this potential scenario.

## Disadvantages to Selling to a Financial Buyer

Since a financial buyer is in it for the money, there are some pretty big disadvantages to selling to them, especially if do not want to sell 100 percent of your company, or if you hope to retain some control:

- **Loss of control.** You will no longer have a say in the direction of the company. Financial buyers are after one thing: money. They will do whatever they can to reach financial objectives, even if it means dropping products and projects that you're passionate about, entire divisions, or team members.

- **Potential clashes with acquiring financial personnel.** The people who acquire your company are focused on financial growth, which means there is potential to clash. Things won't be done the way they were before.

- **Likely required continued employment for you.** The acquiring buyer wants you and the management team to keep growing and scaling the way you have been so they can resell the company. This means they will likely want you and most of the management team to stay on in some role.

- **Noncompete agreements.** In addition to wanting you to stay, the buyer will probably require noncompete agreements from most of your management team, meaning they won't be able to leave and go to a similar company for some time.

- **Risk of being sold off.** If the company underperforms, the buyer will likely sell it quickly after they purchase it, meaning a lot of transition in a short amount of time.

- **Lower cost than a strategic buyer.** Since the buyer essentially wants to flip your company after a few months or years of growth, they aren't going to pay a premium to buy the business.

- **Increased debt risk.** Nearly all financial buyers use debt to acquire companies, which means the buyer is essentially adding debt to your company in order to buy your company. Because of this, your company will have increased debt risk, and will have to continue to meet financial objectives to meet debt repayment.

- **Lower future incentive upsides for selling owners.** While your employees may get financial incentives for reaching future financial milestones, the selling owners likely won't get many incentives after the initial sale as the new owners are looking to grow, scale, and get out.

## What Type of Buyer Will Want Your Company?

Looking at your two lists, you may be getting a pretty solid idea of the type of buyer you want to acquire your company, but certain types of buyers like certain types of companies. So before you start dialing up the CEOs on those two lists, it's helpful to consider the types of companies that strategic and financial buyers often try to acquire. By working through the eighteen steps discussed earlier in this book, you can prepare your company for the buyers you eventually call.

### What Does a Strategic Buyer Look for in a Company?

As we discussed above, the main thing a strategic buyer is looking for is to fill a gap and add value to their current business so they can reach their strategic goals. Their priorities are:

- **Easy integration into existing operations.** Strategic buyers want to buy a company they can quickly integrate into their existing company to increase the current value.

- **Growth.** They may not be looking for huge organic growth, but a strategic buyer wants to acquire companies that have grown consistently and steadily.

- **Access to the management team.** A strategic buyer wants your team as part of the business, so they will look for the ability to talk to and strategize with your current management team.

- **Capabilities expansion.** If you have a product or service that fills a gap in their product line, and acquiring your business allows them to expand their offerings and capabilities, then you are likely a great fit for them.

- **Access to customers and markets**. Oftentimes strategic buyers buy companies to get access to their marketing lists, email lists, and customer base. I have personally acquired media sites just to get the people who are on them, or newsletters just to get the email addresses.

- **Synergies.** Strategic buyers want to gain synergies like equipment, headcount, resources, and purchasing power that they wouldn't otherwise have without buying your company.

- **Industry consolidation.** By increasing its market share in the industry, a company can raise prices and increase profitability. Some strategic buyers look to do this, although I've found that more often than not, it doesn't work out the way they expected.

- **Market, product, or service expansion.** Strategic buyers are looking to acquire companies that will help them to expand into new markets, add to their value ladder, or provide new offerings. If your company fills gaps in those areas, then they will likely be interested.

## What Does a Financial Buyer Look for in a Company?

A financial buyer is looking to add companies to their portfolio that will grow enough in value to give them a strong financial return on investment.

They are interested in:

- **High organic growth.** They want a company that has shown strong growth in the three or four years prior, and they want that growth to be organic through steadily increasing sales.

- **Strong financials.** They want to see that your financials are not only strong, but they have shown growth year-over-year.

- **Leaders in industry.** They want you to be well-respected in your industry and known as someone that people trust as an expert.

- **Potential for acquisitions.** Most buyers supplement organic growth with M&A, so they want to be sure your company can grow through acquisitions.

- **Complement to their existing portfolio.** Financial buyers often buy companies in the same general category or industry. So if a financial buyer acquires media agencies, it's unlikely they will suddenly buy a food manufacturing company.

- **A strong team.** They want to see a robust team in place with experienced managers they can count on to run things.

- **A relatively high moat.** They want some protections in place around your business in terms of differentiated offerings and a large customer base. Basically, they want you to have multiple products and lots of customers.

- **Strong industry.** They want you to be in an industry that has shown strong sales in the years prior, and companies that have the ability to garner a high multiple.

- **A simple CAP table**. They don't want to come into a business with multiple other private equity groups. This makes it too risky and too difficult to manage.

## Now Hone Those Buyer Prospect Lists

At this point, you probably have two lists with a ton of scrawled notes on them. Which list stands out as a better fit for you? Are you more drawn to strategic buyers or financial buyers?

Likewise, which list do you think would be most interested in a company like yours?

You don't have to throw out one of the lists, but at this point, you may want to start ranking the companies on each list according to which ones you think are the best fit. Chances are, several companies will be crossed off, and others may move up in the rankings as more valuable options.

Once you have your list of targeted buyers, it's time to hand that list to your Exit Advisory Team and have them start reaching out.

Because it's time for you to exit that business.

CHAPTER $9$

# EXECUTING YOUR EXIT

Of all the exits I have been involved in, one of my favorites was when we sold our event business, The Traffic & Conversion Summit, to Clarion, a Blackstone company. It was fun because we got to deal with one of the largest private equity funds on the planet, while also dealing with a creative structure, extended negotiations, an evolving business structure, multiple parties with different and sometimes competing interests, and of course, the money. The money was very, very nice.

Every exit is a snowflake because of all the different forces at play, but this deal was especially nice. We did everything right. We assembled our team with me as lead advisor (and also an owner). Our two legal teams, one for the sale transaction and the other for tax planning, provided invaluable help and kept things moving while dealing with sometimes challenging issues from the buyer's legal counsel.

Our accounting team did a fabulous job of recasting financials to reflect the true value of the business. And my partners were supportive, even when they were skeptical about a particular strategy working or not. Their confidence and trust were key to making this what Blackstone and Clarion referred to as the highest multiple they had paid for a business in that industry. We worked through the two most challenging parts of the deal—the covenant not to compete and the working capital adjustment—flawlessly. We were able to secure everything we wanted, from cash retained to the ability to do things post-closing with no real limitations on our ability to work within the industry, even to conduct events.

We were able to separate the event business as the jewel that the buyer wanted and retain our related companies in the marketing, content, event, and logistics space with contracts that continued to support those companies from the event business without losing the personnel, intellectual property, or additional profit centers those supporting companies provided. This is a frequent point of failure. Sellers fail to realize they can sell just what the buyer wants, or they fail to pursue fractionalizing the business for the sale because they don't know how or are afraid that doing so might jeopardize the deal.

In the end, we got everything we wanted. A lot of cash at closing, a lot more cash from an earnout that we were certain we would achieve, highly favored tax treatment from the way the deal was structured, freedom to pursue all the post-closing opportunities we wanted to pursue, and much more. With that, let's begin this closing chapter.

It is time. You've learned all about exits and multiples and risks. You've followed all of the steps to getting your company Exit-Ready. You've learned about types of transactions and exit processes. And you've built a team that's tasked with getting you over the finish line. That end is in sight. It's now time for you to exit.

Before you start opening a bottle of celebratory champagne, I want to take you through the final steps of executing your exit. This is the time when your Exit Advisory Team really starts to shine. They know what they are doing, and they can guide you through the process. Additionally, you can lean on them to advise you when things get complicated, or when you just need someone to talk you off of a ledge.

You're so close, and this is when things finally start to get exciting. Let's get exiting.

## The Exit Process Timeline

In earlier chapters I mentioned that you should begin planning your exit as soon as you start or acquire the business. I also suggested that you start pre-exit planning about two to three years before you actually want to exit. This is when you really dive into the eighteen steps and get your business Exit-Ready. Hopefully, by the time you're reading this chapter, you've done all that and are at the point where you can actually get into the nitty-gritty details of exiting.

There are four phases of actually exiting. As a general rule, the first phase can take anywhere from one month to three years. The next three phases move much faster and should take around five months combined. As with any process, exiting can take longer (especially when a buyer drags the process on) or move quickly if the buyer and seller are both motivated. Here's how that timeline falls:

## Phase One: Pre-Exit Planning and Positioning

A lot of the pre-exit planning and positioning tasks can be done over several months or even years before you actually exit. The timing on these tasks is flexible, and they can be done concurrently, or in any order.

The pre-exit planning and positioning tasks include:

- Estimate a current value

- Research multiple arbitrage opportunities

- Reposition your company for the highest possible multiple

- Do acquisition arbitrage for higher multiples

- Conduct internal due diligence and patched holes

- Researched and prepare a buyer list

During this phase you will also build the big marketing assets that you will use in the process. These assets are complex, and I suggest that you enlist your Exit Advisory Team to help you create them. Otherwise, it will be a long, drawn-out process that will require lots of trial and error.

**Create your initial data room:** As we discussed in chapter 7, this is a secure storage file where you keep all of your pertinent financial and confidential information leading up to an exit. It should be full of any and all information that a potential buyer may want, and should be well-organized so that it's easy for anyone to find what they need.

**Prepare a one-sheet:** This is a short, one-page document that shares the essential information that a buyer wants to know about your company. This one-sheet does not give your company's name or any identifying details. Instead, it simply lists basic industry, regional, geographic information as well as profit range and revenue. For example, it could say:

- Small Midwest manufacturing company with $10 million EBITDA.

- Mid-sized marketing agency with large multinational client base and $12 million EBITDA.

- Large retail clothing store with ten brick-and-mortar locations and a thriving e-commerce site.

**Confidential info memo (CIM):** This is a more in-depth version of your one-sheet that includes confidential information such as your company name. This is only sent once potential buyers have signed a nondisclosure agreement (NDA).

**Prepare a management presentation:** This is an in-depth presentation about your company that is often presented to the buyer by a select team of managers, who are also available for questions and comments.

Once you've finished all the pre-exit planning and positioning, it's time to move on to the more rapid-paced phases of your exit.

## Phase Two: Marketing Round One Bids

This is when your Exit Advisory Team finally gets to reach out to potential buyers and the process really starts to roll. I'm going to break down the next few phases by month so you have a good idea of how quickly the process will happen once you start moving.

**Month One:**

- Buyer outreach with one-sheet
- Dry-runs of management presentation with your management team
- Secure NDAs from any interested desirable buyers

**Month Two:**

- Distribute CIM to desirable buyers who have sent NDA
- Buyers respond with Indication of Interest (IOI)
- Buyers do a first-round bid
- Collect first-round bids

**Month Three (first half):**

- Continue to collect first-round bids and evaluate them

- Select first -round bidders for invitation to management presentation

**Notes on Indications of Interest (IOI)**

- IOI forms can be complex. Here is a little cheat sheet to make sure you understand all the nuances.

- IOI forms are usually required to be received within three weeks of a company receiving the CIM.

- IOI forms are nonbinding.

- Generally, they include a range of potential acquisition valuations on a debt-free, cash-free basis.

- The potential buyer shares anticipated sources of funding in the IOI.

IOI forms are an excellent way to determine how prepared a buyer is to make the acquisition, as well as how serious they are about the acquisition. IOI forms are also a good way to gauge your expectations for potential exit values.

## Phase Three: Select Buyer Second Round Bids

Now the process will really start to move fast. You'll probably have significant disruption to your operations at this point as management will be doing presentations and will need to be available for questions and calls. Still, this phase is short, and your Exit Advisory Team will be able to manage much of it for you.

**Month Three (second half):**

- Deliver bid packages and grant data room access

- Pre-bid due diligence

- Contract markup

**Month Four:**

- Deliver management presentation to selected bidders

- Receive final (second round) bids

- Negotiations and select final bidder

- Confirmatory due diligence

## Phase Four: Close the Sale

At this point, you've chosen a buyer, you've done your presentations, you've received your bids. After some final paperwork, due diligence, and final approvals, it's time to sign and close that deal.

**Month Five:**

- Finalize contract

- Secure all necessary third-party approvals

- Sign and close

## The Phases of the Exit Process

I know this process is complex, so if you need a quick reference to the phases and steps, here you go:

1. A one-sheet, with basic industry, regional, and geographic information, as well as profit range and revenue, is sent to prospective buyers. No

confidential information is sent.

2.  Interested buyers respond and are sent an NDA.

3.  Interested buyers receive Confidential Information Memo (CIM).

4.  Interested buyers respond to CIM with Indication of Interest (IOI).

5.  Company reviews IOIs and determines to which responders it will provide a management presentation.

6.  Company delivers management presentation to interested buyers.

7.  Company selects buyers and enters into IOI.

8.  Sale is closed.

## How to Analyze Prospective Buyers

After you've sent your one-sheet and CIM, you may start to get bids in from prospective buyers. This is a great thing! It means people are interested in your company! It can be a bit overwhelming to go through bids and decide who you want to have move forward in the process. One of the tasks my Exit Advisory Team does is analyze the benefits of each potential buyer in an organic way.

First, I list the potential buyers who have submitted a bid.

Company A

Company B

Company C

Then I write down the major benefits that I want in a potential buyer. For me, those things are:

- Operating expense reduction

- Access to additional markets

- Cross-selling possibility

- Tech stack advantages and capabilities

- Access to operations teams

- Access to development teams

I give each company one point for each item they fulfill from my benefits list. So if Company A offers a reduction in operating expenses, and a cross-selling possibility, but nothing else, then their score is 2 out of 6. If Company B has everything other than access to operations teams, then they score 5 out of 6.

Your list of benefits may be different from mine. Maybe you're looking for access to manufacturing, or a storefront, or a media-buying team, or a certain product line, or a willingness to let go of certain divisions. Whatever it is, list out your benefits, and then simply rank your potential bids based on how many of the important benefits they have.

Two other factors to look at are their capacity to pay and their history of acquisitions. If the company has sketchy financials and has never acquired before, they may not be as desirable as a company that has made several acquisitions and historically shown strong financials.

You can do all the analysis in the world and rank and rate these potential buyers, but the truth is there will likely be some amazing benefits to each company, as well as some downsides. For me, it often comes down to a gut instinct:

- Which buyer did I mesh with best? (This is especially important if you're maintaining an equity stake or staying on to help during the transition.)
- Which buyer seemed to align most with my strategic vision?
- Which buyer seemed the most passionate about the acquisition and wants it the most?
- Which one will treat my employees the best in the future?
- Which one makes me most excited when I hear their vision?

All of these gut questions can be key determinates of who you ultimately choose.

## Make Your Choice and Celebrate

This moment may feel a bit anticlimactic because making an exit is a lot of work. You've probably been living and breathing the idea for months, if not years, and when you get to the point where you say, "Yes, this is what I want. I want Company B to buy my business!" it can come with a whole range of thoughts and emotions.

*Finally! It's done.*

*I can't believe it's over.*

*Let's hit the beach.*

*I'm so tired.*

*I am not sure I want to go.*

*I can't wait to get out of here.*

*Did I make the right choice?*

*I most definitely made the right choice.*

*I did it.*

*We did it.*

*Finally, it's done!*

Making an exit is a big thing—a *huge* thing. It's all of the work you've done in the last several years wrapped up in a culminating event. That event likely has a big red bow on it in the form of a hefty payday.

Whatever you are feeling, I encourage you to stay in the emotions for a while. It's okay to feel happy and sad and scared and excited and nervous and exuberant all at once. It's okay to already be thinking about what you want to do next, and it's also okay to never think about running a business again. It's okay to open the champagne, to book those tickets to Italy, to buy that car. It's also okay to put the money in the bank and pretend nothing has changed.

The point is, this is your exit. It was your business, your plan, your move. You can handle it in whatever way you think is best. But whatever you do, do one thing: Celebrate the fact that you did it.

You built a business that had enough value to be worth buying. You created products and operating systems and teams that worked. You increased your value, built an exit team, and managed the exit process.

You exited.

Congratulations.

# APPENDIX: SOME FINAL ADVICE ON EXITING

As I mentioned before, mergers, acquisitions, and owner exits are kind of my thing. While my original trade was as an entrepreneur starting and owning several businesses, I eventually saw that it was far easier to acquire existing successful businesses than to start them from scratch.

I evolved to acquiring and selling businesses myself for my own account, and then helped thousands of others as an attorney for well over a decade, but I'm really an entrepreneur at heart. After building several businesses, acquiring others through M&A, and then exiting several, I realized that my passion lies in helping other founders build, grow, acquire, and exit businesses. I love helping owners reach their objectives and get the most they can out of their businesses. And I love helping those same owners get into the M&A game and build, grow, acquire, and exit again and again.

This book is designed to be a high-level view of the Exit-Ready Process. If you want more advice, more information, or more coaching, I invite you to visit https://Scalable.co/ExitReadyResources. On the site, you'll find several helpful tools that supplement the content of this book as well as access to information about products and services that are designed to give you actionable tools and strategies to help you profit from change.

These includes:

**Exit-Ready Coaching Program.** We offer a range of exit coaching and consulting packages, including one-on-one mentorship, recorded workshops, tools, and more.

**The EPIC Challenge.** A LIVE five-day training event that walks you through the entire process of acquiring highly profitable businesses, traffic channels, or assets with zero money out of pocket.

**The EPIC Business Buyer Basic and Advanced Acquisitions Programs.** Intense, eight-week coaching and personalized mentorship programs where you'll have the opportunity to work hand-in-hand with Roland and his team of merger and acquisition experts as they guide you through each step of the process toward acquiring your own profitable businesses, traffic channels, or assets.

**EPIC Board.** EPIC Board members enjoy three in-person private events per year, weekly live mentorship, private quarterly mastermind sessions, access to private member-only resources, high-value connections, special perks, and much more.

**Scale & Exit.** Our bespoke partnership program where we link arms with you over a period of one to five years to get your business Exit-Ready and actually conduct the full exit process for you.

**HelloExit.** Our exit and acquisition brokerage that runs the exit process for you.

I look forward to connecting with you!

www.ingramcontent.com/pod-product-compliance
Lightning Source LLC
Chambersburg PA
CBHW031846200326
41597CB00012B/289